A Sabbath Rest

A FORTY DAY DEVOTIONAL

DENNIS J. GALLAHER

The Sabbath is a means of grace, the Sabbath is a Divine provision by which man can have help and strength and blessing, not something by which he is to be bound, and fastened and burdened. The Sabbath is that through which God in infinite love would cheer the drooping heart of humanity; and it is the Son of Man, the master of men, who is the Lord and Master of the Sabbath. — G. Campbell Morgan

Several of the photographs included in this publication are courtesy of True Vineyard Ministries, a Christian organization providing holistic support to Rwanda's poorest through job creation, community building, and Christian counsel. TVM envisions Africa's most vulnerable people transformed into healthy, prosperous, and collaborative communities of social change through Jesus Christ. To find out more about this ministry visit www.truevineyard.org

To Jan,

My heart always trusts in you, and I have had no lack all of these days.
Many others have done well but you exceed them all. You have always
feared God and loved me, and for that I am most grateful.
Because of you, I am a blessed man.

Acknowledgements

Thank You, Father, for providing the great gift of Sabbath rest to us.
Thank you for Your covenant promises that take me through all of life.
Thank you, Jesus, for befriending me, being my Lord, saving me and
always being with me. Thank you, Holy Spirit, for always being present in
both the difficulties and the blessings. You are awesome.

Thank you, Terri Snead, for your partnership and expertise in doing
what I do not do well. Your skill makes theory into practice. Your "Family
Time" exercises will bless the generations.

Thank you, Travis Keas. Your exuberance and servant heart energizes me.
Your layout work and graphics are a touch of grace to this project.

Thank you, Abbey Henderson, for your pictures and editing skill. You are
a joy to be creative with and your photos are filled with Godly passion.

Thank you Freedom Fellowship. You have been journey-mates with Jan
and me for many years. Your care and partnership is a constant source of
inspiration.

May you all enter into the joy of the Father's rest.

Foreword

Our first child, a beautiful baby girl named Cheri, was everything a young couple could desire. However, she could sometimes cry herself into an angry, almost hysterical state. We were inexperienced first parents at best and would try everything to stop the thrashing and increasingly out of control crying. It didn't take long to learn to hold her very tightly against our chest and just walked with her. Eventually, the flailing arms would relax and little Cheri would gradually rest peacefully against our chest.

Our word "religion" comes from a Latin source, "religio," which means "to tie or fasten," but perhaps the best definition is "to bind back." It is the picture of a surgeon who repairs a ligament by binding the tear back together.

Now, some folk would hear that and say, "I get it. Religion binds us – it's legalistic and uncomfortable. I need to be free!" And thus they continue flailing themselves through life experiences. Like little Cheri, they thrash and kick, never reaching a place of real rest.

But the key understanding is this. True religion "binds us back" to a relationship of love and purpose with the key Person of true love, our great God and Savior, Jesus Christ. There we relax to find a relationship, safe, strong and full of loving purpose, in the Person of true life, Jesus Christ.

The Old Testament reveals our Father's early dealings with His people and shows a clear pattern of paternal wisdom. He vulnerably chose to dwell among His people giving them specific laws for enriched living, including a place where He would dwell among them, an organized leadership from among their own ranks, and important worship requirement to include feasts, celebrations and disciplines for each year. In short, Israel was being made ready to effectively worship and serve God, receiving the joy and blessings of being a special people. The people of God, like every nation, needed special days to celebrate their national existence and freedom.

God was continually "binding back" a people to Himself. Through regular reminders of redemption, cleansing and consecration, along with the infilling of supernatural strength in the Holy Spirit, they were made into a witness of divine hope and providence while they waited in God's presence.

And the foundation of all that experience in God, the keystone of true purpose in the calling and completion of new life, was the Sabbath (Leviticus 23:1-3). It revealed the hope of final perfection and the experience of walking in God's revealed presence.

In the New Testament, Hebrews 4 teaches us that each believer can experience this Sabbath, which is the promise of the true and complete rest of God, by believing fully in the provision made through our Lord Jesus Christ.

> *"So there is a special rest still waiting for the people of God...*
> *so let us do our best to enter into that rest." Hebrews 4:9,13 NLT*

Our Pastor and leadership wisely plan a time for a practical Sabbath every year. It is an applied and experiential fulfillment of being released and set free, while being bound tightly to a life of spiritual rest—the Sabbath of the Lord. All of us should do the same, not in the legalistic boundaries of rules and regulations but in the freedom of the Sabbath that Jesus promised. Be blessed, fellow traveler, and enter into His rest.

Pastor Rick C. Howard, pastor and author

A Note From The Author

Eighteen minutes before sundown, a trumpet blast sounded throughout the nineteenth century Jewish ghetto. Sabbath was about to begin. A devout wife would drop a few coins, often desperately needed to buy bread for the children, into her pushkah, which was her private charity coin-box.

What would follow the clink of the coins in the little box was tradition handed down from mother to daughter for generations. Standing over the unlit Sabbath candles, she would close her eyes and place her fingers over them to shut out the physical reminders of the worldly life. With devout reverence for this most holy of days, the words of this prayer were uttered to God;

> *"Blessed are thou, O Lord our God, King of the Universe,*
> *Who has sanctified us by Thy commandments,*
> *and has commanded us to kindle the Sabbath lights."*

With this solemn and holy benediction she would beseech God with the prayer of her heart for His divine blessing on her husband and children. After this most holy yet simple of preparations the Sabbath lights would be lit.

Sabbath had begun. For twenty-four hours, the most oppressed and despised people group on the earth honored God through rest.

Meanwhile, the local synagogue filled with men at the Sabbath Eve service. The head of each family would leave the service with one of the poor men of the community and walk the few blocks to his home. The poor man would be an honored guest throughout the Sabbath and would join the family in all of the celebration. No matter that the meal would be simple and the bed hard. The family would make up for the lack with the warmth of brotherhood extended to a fellow Jew.

The streets would be filled with the familiar smells of Sabbath that poured from every kitchen in the ghetto. As each man entered his home, his children would present themselves to receive their Sabbath blessing, the same blessing that Jacob pronounced over his grandsons, Ephraim and Manasseh.

But the most touching event was yet to take place. At a time chosen by the head of the house, all would gather around his helpmate, the devoted wife and mother, who was the key to the Sabbath's joy. He would then sing in honor of his wife the hymn Eishes Chayil meaning "A Good Woman." Taken from the Book of Proverbs, the words reveal the high esteem that elevated the role of women among the Jews.

Strength and dignity are her clothing…
She openeth her mouth with wisdom;
And the law of kindness is on her tongue…
Her children rise up, and call her blessed;
Her husband also, and he praiseth her.

Oh, Sabbath! For the Jewish nation scattered throughout the world it has been the strong bond that has continually reminded them of Jehovah's love and care. Each Sabbath was the reminder that they remained the apple of His eye.

And that brings us to today. Throughout the Bible, the people of God have had a standing invitation as well as a command to enter into the unique blessing of the Sabbath. It is a time to renew and deepen all of our relationships, especially with those who are poor of spirit and lonely of heart. It is a time to remember that we are a part of a larger community and do not function apart from one another. It is a time for deepening the love of family.

In other words, as parents took time to bless their children, this season will provide ample time to do the same. For busy families, the Sabbath rest will supply you with new opportunities to bless your children with the most precious gift of all— your time and attention.

There is also the greatest of all Sabbath blessings. In the blessing of our sisters in the Lord (especially the husband blessing their wife) lies the hidden mysteries of our Lord's love relationship with us, His church.

Forty days from now your Sabbath will draw to a close. I pray that as the shadows grow long on this Sabbath rest so will your heartfelt understanding of entering into the Sabbath of the Lord.

May you be blessed in the Lord's Rest.

Table Of Contents

How to Use This Devotional

My hope is that over these next forty days you will do more than simply read this devotional. As a part of this season of rest, I want to encourage you to engage in the following disciplines beyond the devotional.

- Everyday, you will find activities to talk with children and teens about God's gift of Sabbath. Use the "Family Time" suggestions to talk to your kids around the dinner table, before bedtime or riding in the car.

- Have you ever journaled before? These next forty days, write down your thoughts and prayers in the "Selah" section. It will be a blessing to you to go back later and read what the Lord taught you.

- Recite the Lord's Prayer everyday and consider taking communion on a regular basis throughout this time. Both of these disciplines will take on a new significance as you embrace them over these days.

Any season of Sabbath is founded on the desire to draw close to God. Drawing close to someone means intimate communication and the sharing of heartfelt joys as well as the deep concerns that this life brings. It is no different when we set aside extended periods of Sabbath to renew our friendship with God and our passion for prayer and time alone with the Lord.

Sabbath must begin with prayer, and prayer begins by listening to the instructions of the Master as He taught us to pray. To begin this time of Sabbath, read and pray the great prayer of instruction that Jesus taught us from Matthew 6:9-13 and Luke 11:2-4.

The Lord's Prayer is a template for effective prayer in a believer's life. Seven topics that are essential for life in the Spirit are profoundly noted by the Lord as He teaches us the basics of communion with the Father. Jesus taught us to pray for each one daily, so begin this season with prayer and meditation through the Lord's Prayer.

Lets get started. Take a nice, deep breath. Sing your favorite worship song. Say the Lord's Prayer. Welcome to the Sabbath, God's divine rest.

Introduction

"So there remains a Sabbath rest for the people of God." (Hebrews 4:9 NASB)

"How did it get so late so soon?" (Dr. Seuss)

It was dark when the first text of the day came in. The ding, and then another ding, and then another ding, were unusual but not surprising. Texts, those hot shot messages that we send through outer space to one another at a maddening pace, are still better than phone calls before six am. Their arrival left no doubt that the day had started. I needed to be at the hospital before nine, return an emergency phone call before that, feed the dogs, look at the plants, kiss my wife, and leave.

Time has become one of the most precious commodities in the world even though it is completely inflexible. It neither grows nor shrinks; it cannot be expanded or contracted, and it has no growth fund where it can be invested. No matter what you do, not one second will ever be added to the clock and not one second taken away; the problem not being the clock, but all the "stuff" that is stuffed into the time we have.

Because it never changes, time is uniquely simple. No matter where in the world the clock ticks, it is married to the same cadence of the spinning globe we live on. The sunrise and sunset can be pinpointed to a hair's breath, all because time does not change. It is one of the most constant, stable and guaranteed standards—since time began.

To understand how significant time is, you must go back to the Garden: not to the Fall of Adam and Eve, but back further still; back to the new day story; back to miraculous simplicity of creation.

- Five days and then the sixth.

- Adam formed by God the Sculptor and born from the earth.

- Fashioned and then divine breath, the Spirit of God, breathed in, "and man became a living soul."

Most would conclude creation had ended with the sixth day of creation and now it was time for God to rest. Not so; another day, Day Seven, and God created still.

"And on the seventh day God ended His work…" (Gen. 2:2 NKJV)

The great Jewish scholar, Rabbi Shlomo Yitzchaki (1040-1105 A.D.), explains. To this day, he is known for his concise ability to uncomplicate the Jewish scriptures while staying true to the text. Writing just beyond the first century his works remain a centerpiece of contemporary Jewish study. Concerning that seventh day, he wrote,

*Nathan Ausubel, The Book of Jewish Knowledge (New York: Crown, 1964), 378.

"What was created on the seventh day? It is found in the second part of the verse...*He rested on the seventh day from all His work which He had done.*"*

Creation was not complete until rest was created. Sabbath, the name for the seventh day of creation, was not the creation, but the vessel. What was created was the first lesson taught to Adam; on that first day of his life, he rested with God.

The old Jewish sages were convinced that rest was never to end. Adam and Eve's destiny was meant to be a continuous place of rest with the Creator. Those sages pointed out that every other day ended with "there was evening and there was morning," but not the seventh day. Instead the final note on that day was He rested; and that rest was to continue throughout the good life planned for God's children.

The world was created in perfection; God's wisdom dictating every detail, so the phrase "evening and morning" and the twenty-four hours that it represents were part and parcel to the perfection. God's intention was for man to submit his own life to the order of perfection created.

Enter the Fall, the abuse of perfection by Adam and Eve. Enter the destruction and desecration of God's great gifts of life, freedom, intimacy and care. With sin comes the pride that refuses responsibility while demanding that God change, not sinful man. In other words, the blindness of sin results in the blaming of God's order instead of the breaking of man's rebellion against God. And when it comes to the order of God of evening and morning, man has done everything possible to not conform to God's plan.

You can't change time. It is the one inflexible that can be counted on... every day, hour, minute, second. You can count on it like clockwork.

The beginning of creation's story and the absolute rebellion that made God's perfect order the nemesis of mankind's rebellion was not the end of the story though. Within God's perfect order was another unique part of time. On that seventh day God created rest which is the translation for the Hebrew word "menucha", rich in understanding and context. It is first used in Genesis 2:2 (NASB), "*...and He rested [menucha] on the seventh day from all His work which He had done.*"

It wasn't until the Exodus that the day became known as the Sabbath. God speaks and says, "*...Tomorrow is to be a day of Sabbath rest, a holy Sabbath to the Lord... (Exodus 16:23 NIV)*"

Shabbat, the Hebrew word for Sabbath, means "stop." The two words joined together give a clear and absolute portrait in living color of God's intentions for His new creation—*shabbat menucha,* stop and rest.

What was lost at the fall of Adam and Eve? Everything, including *menucha.* Talk about a loss. What ended at the fall went all the way back to the breath of God and the first gift to man. All of it. Gone.

Look at the Gate of Eden. Broken and enslaved mankind was driven from the perfection God had planned. Imagine the stripping away of all of God's good gifts left piled just on the inside of the Gate. Like the wagon trains that unloaded their treasures as they trekked across the unrelenting deserts, the treasures lie until the sands hid and destroyed them. On the outside, the land was cursed. Beyond the flaming sword that guarded the path back, toil, thorns and thistles tore at the still warm skins laid on the backs of the children now separated from their former home.

Millennia pass. God speaks of His rest and even commands His people to receive. The command becomes another form of man's rebellion and is eventually entangled by man's rules and regulations. His desire to be independent and to rule the seventh day that God created loaded his back to breaking and calloused his heart.

The true rest that God had promised was only a word until the God who created it for His children spoke again to the sons of Adam through Jesus. It was a day of revelation. Jesus was pouring out truth to those who had ears to hear (Matthew 11:15 NASB). And then the promise of the Garden is spoken. The long-lost gift is returned.

> *"Come unto Me, all who are weary and heavy-laden,*
> *and I will give you rest." (Matt. 11:28 NASB)*

The rest, the true Sabbath of God, would return when man was once again at peace with his Maker. The night of the resurrection, the risen Jesus appears to the terrified and over-burdened crew of disciples and commands the souls of the disciples to come alive in the same fashion as the first.

> *"...He breathed on them and said to them, 'Receive the Holy Spirit.'" (John 20:22 NASB)*

With that, the Garden promise of rest became a reality. The gift was restored as the Son of God made peace with the Father for us. For me. For you. The seventh day restored,

> *"So there remains a Sabbath rest for the people of God. For the one who has entered His rest has himself also rested from his works, as God did from His. Therefore let us be diligent to enter that rest, so that no one will fall, through following the same example of disobedience." (Heb. 4:9-11 NASB)*

Sabbath is the answer; a Sabbath rest for the people of God. Sabbath is not a break once a week, a vacation or a "mental health day." Sabbath is a lifestyle that must be entered into with diligence and obedience.

One of the most discussed topics in both the Old and New Testament (mentioned sixty-six times in the Old Testament and fifty-six times in the New Testament), Sabbath is, by and large, considered an legalistic tenant that is long past its due date. Could it be that God desires with all of His heart to return a truth to all, both believer and unbeliever, that rest and peace can be found only in Jesus Christ? Just a thought…

So welcome to A Sabbath Rest. This is not a task to be completed or even a well designed manual of study, but an invitation to gain something so valuable that it was the first gift beyond life given to Adam and the first gift beyond salvation returned by the second Adam.

Go back to the Garden. Hear the words, *"Come unto Me."* Resist the drum beat that signals business as usual. Enter the Father's world where He rested from His own works and sit with Him awhile.

It is there that you will find Sabbath rest, *Shabbat menucha,* for your soul.

Day One

"Remember your last name," I would say as he stood in the open door ready to leave for the evening. Teenagers have a tendency to forget who they are without the presence of parents and so I would repeat that phrase every time he would leave. "Remember your last name."

- Remember I have the same name.

- Remember lots of people know who I am.

- Remember that our name represents all of us, not just you.

And off he would go, remembering that our name meant something and was to be protected from the harm of bad behavior.

Jesus said that the Father's name was "hallowed" which means holy, sacred, revered, worshiped. And we are to begin our talks with Him by remembering that the Name means something and that I am to protect and honor it by my behavior.

There is a beautiful name in the Hebrew language for Father. It is the name *Abba,* which is equivalent to the term *dear father* or *dad*. Jesus used it in the Garden when He cried out, "Abba, let this cup pass... but not My will but Thine be done." Tenderly spoken at a point of complete trust, the Savior approached the holiness of God with the affection of a much loved child.

It is the same word that Paul used when he wrote to us, *"For you did not receive the spirit of bondage again to fear, but you received the Spirit of adoption by whom we cry out, 'Abba, Father.'* (Romans 8:15 NKJV; italics added)"

Because of the great love of the Father, I approach the throne of holiness with both reverent awe and unflinching safety. His very name is sacred, let alone the essence of His glory. But in my heart, I reach out to Him with a name that eclipses all others. This great God who created this world as well as that secret place in my heart where He dwells is first and foremost my Abba.

And I will not forget His name.

Family Time

Tell each child the story of how and why you decided upon their name. Make this a time of celebration of each child's unique and special identity.

Next, tell a story about a time when you knew the God of the universe was taking care of you – just like a loving father would care for his children. You might start your story with these words,

"There was a time when I knew God loved me like a dad, and that was when *(blank)*."

O, Abba, open my eyes this early morning so that I might worship You face to face. Abba, You are in Heaven and I am on the earth. Your Name is revered and holy. As I go about my tasks here on earth today, I will not forget Your Name and that my actions represent You.

Selah

Day Two

"Thy Kingdom come." (Matt. 6:10 KJV)

Sometimes, all I want to do is escape. Whether it is a conversation or a location, my mind goes into overdrive looking for the road that got me there so I can hit reverse and back out as quickly as I arrived.

On the other hand, Jesus chose to stay. Within hours of His departure through the Via Dolorosa, He remarked to Pilate that this world was not His home. Beyond the physical location, He stated to Pilate that nothing in this world even resembled the Kingdom he ruled, "If My Kingdom was of this world, My servants would be fighting..." In other words, everything about this world is crude and rudimentary when held up to the light of God's Kingdom.

Jesus instructs His church to pray to the Father first and foremost, "Thy Kingdom Come!" Each day, the light of Godly wisdom that snuffs out the crude ways of this world needs to flow from my life. This world's ways cannot even comprehend the ways of the Kingdom of Heaven let alone match them step for step. This world's ways are eclipsed by the Kingdom when lived out by the saints of God.

It would not be too many days from the cross when Christians stood prayerfully still while being pounded to death with stones. They were hung on crosses and covered with pitch to be set on fire. Why did they not fight back? Why did they not demand respect? Why did they not stop stirring the pot with their preaching? It is simple.

The Kingdom for which they had been taught to pray had come into their lives. The principles of the King had eclipsed the crude tenants of this world. And now those who knew Him knew His Kingdom ways as well.

I wonder what would happen if we did the same?

Family Time

Talk about the fairy tales that take place in a kingdom or discuss what life is like for members of royal families today. What special privileges come with royalty? What special responsibilities come with royalty?

Next, tell your kids about the gratitude that comes when you are member of God's Kingdom. Talk about your personal thankfulness - that since you are a member of God's royal family:

- You have been blessed with every spiritual blessing.

- You have confidence that nothing can separate you from God's family.

- You have a God who provides all your needs.

Finally, tell your children about how this same gratitude makes you want to live a life of Kingdom focus. Your words might sound like: "I am so grateful I am a part of God's Kingdom because *(blank)*. Since I am a part of God's Kingdom, I want my life to *(blank)*."

Lord, open my blind eyes that I might catch a glimpse of Your Kingdom today! Let me see the glory of following You and being like You. And when those around me throw stones and insults, send Your Holy Spirit to remind me of Your words. I want to be like You and not like the world today.

Day Three

"Thy will be done on earth as it is in Heaven." (Matt. 6:10 KJV)

Jesus didn't settle for "good enough" and He expects the same from you. In other words, only settle for Heaven's best.

We used to have only one big grocery store in town. The Texas grocer, H.E.B., recognized the growth of the town and planted another one, bigger and better, on the other side of town, same grocer but two different stores. The new store is only a ten-minute drive from the original but a world away in size and choices. Now that is something to celebrate in small town, USA!

But all of a sudden, the quality of the original store noticeably declined. No more organic produce. More lower end bargain foods. Fewer cashiers and now you bag most of your own groceries. Some people in town just got used to it; they would complain, mind you, but that is where they shopped and they sure were not going to "drive all the way to the other side of town" to go to the big, new store, ten whole minutes to the west.

Now, I don't mean to confuse you but isn't that the way a lot of people pray? "On earth as it is in Heaven" as long as it doesn't take too long or cost too much or (God forbid!) require me to discipline my life. And if it does? I'll complain but in the end settle for "good enough" instead of contending for "Heaven's best."

Paul said, "I press on towards the goal for the prize of the upward call of God in Christ Jesus (Philippians 3:14 NASB)."

Refuse to settle for even the best this world has to offer. Settle for nothing less than the prize Jesus Christ won for me. Thy will be done, Abba. Just like it is in Heaven, let it be here on the earth.

Family Time

Selah

Ask each family member to think about the best prize or award they have ever received. Remember these moments with one another and celebrate together. "The best prize or award that I've received was *(blank)*, and I loved it because *(blank)*."

Read the story of Christ's baptism in Matthew three. Jesus received the ultimate honor (or prize) from God when the heavens opened and God announced how proud He was of His Son. God is just as proud of you and me! Imagine what it would be like for God to open up the clouds and say the same words about you. Talk about how your life might be different if you really, really believed God felt this way about you. "If God opened up the clouds and announced He was proud of me, I would feel *(blank)*. I think my life here on earth might look a little different because *(blank)*."

Abba, I want Your will and nothing less in my life today. I confess that I so often walk in darkness that I do not know what You want! Please, Father, by the awesome power of Your Holy Spirit, lead me in Your ways today.

Day Four

"Give us this day our daily bread." (Matt. 6:11 NASB)

Daily bread is a big deal in every corner of the world. Whether it is roti (Indian), tortillas (South America), chapatis (Africa), soda bread (Ireland), or good old American ButterCrust, bread is a staple of life.

For the Jewish culture, "daily bread" meant something else as well. The divine bread of the wilderness was called "manna" meaning, "what's that?" I'm not kidding. Tradition says that when they noticed this strange stuff falling from the sky, they looked at each other and said, "What is that stuff?" I suppose you could say they just looked at each other and said, "Manna?!" And so manna became their daily bread. It was God-supplied. Heaven-sent. No one really knew what to call it because no one had ever seen it.

When Jesus told the disciples to pray that God would give them daily bread, it was two-fold. Certainly they would need daily physical substance. Everyone needs to eat. But just like their ancestors who wandered in a God-ordained wilderness, the disciples would also be striking out into new territory and to a Promised Land of Kingdom living. Jesus' words were not just about bread but about a Kingdom way of life, trusting God to supply daily the amazing grace needed to fill the soul with divine nourishment.

Most likely, your pantry is full today, and your refrigerator packed with those little Styrofoam boxes of left-overs from last night. You do not need the daily bread of this world. But what about some amazing grace for today? What about the fresh manna of His Word? What about the tender and small Voice that says, "This is the way. Walk ye therein." Isn't your soul hungry for a taste of Kingdom living and truth?

I'm getting hungry just thinking about it. How about you?

Family Time

Selah

Talk to one another about some of the best meals you've ever eaten. Reminisce about some of your favorite memories involving food. You might even start your stories this way: "Life would be terrific, if I had an endless supply of *(blank)* because *(blank)*." Or, "Life would be perfect, if I never ran out of *(blank)* because *(blank)*."

Next, talk about how we have a Heavenly Father who is our ultimate supply of everything we need. If we need more patience, He's got plenty of it. If we need more forgiveness, God's never in short supply. If we need more kindness, we can go to the God who *is* love.

Share your responses with one another: "I need more of God's *(blank)* today because *(blank)*."

(For example: I need more of God's compassion today because there is a person at work who is hard to love.) End your discussion with prayer. Tell God that you need more of His daily supply.

Abba, I am hungry for Your Word today. I am hungry for Your marvelous banquet of Holy Spirit fruit in my life! Please, Lord, give me today the manna of righteousness that You promised in Your Word.

Day Five

"And forgive us our debts, as we also have forgiven our debtors." (Matt. 6:12 NASB)

I wonder why He did not tell us to pray, "Forgive us our sins"?

The word is "debts." Something owed that had not been paid. Not one something, mind you, but many. Plural. So many debts that it was overwhelming and it was either forgiveness or bankruptcy.

Have you ever had a debt forgiven? Has anyone you tried to pay back looked you in the eye and said, "Forget it. We're square. Go take the family out to dinner and a movie on me." That doesn't happen unless you know someone well.

On the other hand, the banker doesn't do that. The banker has a job to do and it is called debt collection. His words are different and usually written on very formal business letters that say things like, "Overdue. Pay up now. Penalties assessed." I have a relationship with both bankers and friends, but a very different relationship no doubt.

But there is more. The word in the original language is opheiletes and means "one who owes a moral obligation." Another place in the bible the word is translated as "sinner." In our language, the word would be used to describe a criminal who needs to pay his debt to society. Go to jail. Pay the fine. Have your name listed in the local paper so everyone can see that you owe a debt to all the rest of us.

Jesus says, "Pray to the Father and ask Him to forgive those moral bills you can't pay. Then turn around and do the same to others." He was telling them to do something they had never done before. Asking to be forgiven is one thing. Asking to be released from the debt is something else entirely. Forgive others the same way? Unheard of!

An old song went like this,
He paid a debt He did not owe;
I owed a debt I could not pay;
I needed someone to wash my sins away.
And, now, I sing a brand new song,
"Amazing Grace."
Christ Jesus paid a debt
That I could never pay.

Every day, the Father offers to clean the slate and start fresh. That's called an offer I should never refuse.

Family Time

Selah

Tell your children the story of the day they were born. Talk about your stay in the hospital, what the environment was like, what a joy it was to finally get to meet their precious child. Next, present each child with a "bill" for his or her stay in the hospital. Explain the medical costs associated with childbirth and then express your "pretend" expectation of their repayment. Talk about how this debt is theirs to pay. When your kids object, make the following point.

All of us have a debt we cannot pay. We all make choices that go against God's perfect will. Tell your children about your gratitude for how Christ has paid your debt. Talk about your debt of moral obligation and how glad you are that Jesus paid what you could not. Then pray together as a family. "God, I know that my sins and my wrong choices are like a bill that I could not pay. Jesus took my bill and paid it for me. I am so grateful because *(blank)*."

Father, today I receive Your rest as the great gift You promised it would be. I will rest in You and with You today, Lord. I will trust you, Lord, as You pour out Your blessings today, open my eyes to see Your glory!

Day Six

"Lead us not into temptation but deliver us from evil." (Matt. 6:13 KJV)

"Jesus was led by the Spirit into the wilderness to be tempted by the devil (Matt. 4:1 NKJV)."

"He learned obedience through the things that He suffered (Heb. 5:8 NASB)."

He knew I would never be able to take it. He knew that a frontal assault by the devil would destroy any improvement accomplished in me by the work of the Holy Spirit. He knew that in my own strength I could never sustain the holiness and tenacity that would stand in the face of hell itself. So He told me to pray, "Abba, please, today, do not lead me to the den of the devourer. Instead, deliver me from all sorts of evil he plans."

I am greatly humbled by this. It is early morning and the sun has not risen. The day is fresh and new. The sun is slowly pushing the darkness away as the earth rolls into the light of the day. If this request is not fulfilled, the enemy's hateful schemes will envelop my day. That is why Jesus tells me to pray, "Lead me not into the temptations alone. Lend me Your great grace in the trials I will face today."

"He gives grace to the humble (Prov. 3:34 NKJV)."

There is another scene of great temptation played out in the life of the Master. These two are bookends of His faith-filled life here on earth. The Wilderness Temptation was one while the Garden Temptation was the other that declares His trust and submission to the Father's plan. In the Garden we hear these words, *"...nevertheless not my will, but Thine be done (Luke 22:42 KJV)."*

Jesus left a memorial of faithful prayers throughout His life for us to pray today. He knew we could not pray well, so He taught us not only how but what to pray. So this morning and throughout this day I have the confidence to say "lead me not" instead of "bring it on," or "I can take it." Because I cannot. I will fail without His grace.

So Father, don't lead me where Jesus went for me. Give me grace instead. Not my will, but Thine be done!

Family Time

Selah

Ask your kids to complete some sort of physical challenge you know is impossible for them to do alone. *(For example: use a can opener to open a can of food – using only one hand)*. Before too much frustration sets in, ask each child if they would like some help. Point out how much more success is experienced when we humbly ask for help.

Next, discuss how impossible it is for us to live perfect lives. Tell your children about one area in which you ask for Christ's help on a regular basis (In this area, you know that you can't do it alone, but with Christ's help and grace you have victory). Talk about how amazing it is that we have a God who doesn't just tell us or want us to live holy lives, He shows us how. He models the need for humbly asking for help and then empowers us with His presence. Pray together as a family. Encourage each person to ask for God's help in a particular area of their life.

Abba, wherever You lead, You give the grace to follow. Whatever path I find myself on today whether it be blessing or trial, You are with me! You told me in Your Word that You give Your angels charge over me to carry me through all my ways. I humbly submit to Your care today, Father. Thank You that where You lead, You give the grace to follow.

12

Day Seven

"Do not fear, little flock, for it is your Father's good pleasure to give you the Kingdom (Luke 12:32 NKJV)."

This prayer is directed to the Father, but the trinity of the Son and the Holy Spirit is not excluded. The Kingdom belongs to the Father, the Power is the Holy Spirit and the Glory goes to the Lord Jesus Christ. And Jesus, the glorious Lord that is magnified through His sacrifice, promises that the great and everlasting Kingdom of God will be given to you and I. No strings attached. Lock, stock and barrel. The keys to His Kingdom being handed over to me with joy from the Father.

Jesus said, *"I will give you the keys of the kingdom of heaven, and whatever you bind on earth will be bound in heaven, and whatever you loose on earth will be loosed in heaven (Matthew 16:19)."*

The explanation is simple. Whoever has the keys has the control and the authority. The saints of God have been given the power to forbid sin from going forward as well as the power to loose the power of God wherever they choose. And that's just the tip of the iceberg. You will never plunge the awesome power of the Kingdom this side of eternity. So high you can't get over it. So low you can't get under it. So wide you can't get around it. That just rocks my soul.

Do you realize what great love and trust the Father must have for His church to do this? Without a doubt, the keys to the Kingdom represent the greatest of benefits that the child of God could imagine. And every day, every time we approach the Father, we end with these wonderful promises that secure everything that has proceeded this final declaration.

When you declare that "the Kingdom, the power and the glory" belong to the Father, you are rehearsing the very gifts released to you as well. Don't just sit there. Get out the keys and open the treasure chest of Kingdom promises as well as the great love of the Father. After all, the last thing my day needs is another locked door. Don't leave the keys behind today. Go and open the door of the Kingdom in your world today.

"Behold what manner of love the Father has bestowed on us, that we should be called children of God (1 John 3:1 NKJV)!"

Family Time

Show your children examples of how having the right key or having the right password will allow access to all kinds of "riches." Show young children how having the right key will allow access to all the toys in their room. Discuss how having the right password can access bank accounts, cell phones and computers.

Next, explain that our Heavenly Father offers all of His children access to the riches of His Kingdom. If we are children of God's family, then He is excited (pleased) to give us the blessings of His grace. Remind your children about some of the blessings/riches of God's Kingdom. Share your amazement and gratitude for our generous Heavenly Father.

Father, today I hold in my hands the keys to Your Kingdom, Your power and Your glory. I confess that I don't fully understand the power that You have given to me. Today, show me how to use these to take Your Kingdom forth.

Selah

14

Day Eight

Sabbath...The seventh day of the week as well as certain feast days marked in ancient Israel, Judaism, and early Christianity by cessation of work and ceremonial observance.

When God creates something, only man's rebellion can change it. For centuries the natural rhythm of life declared that God was indeed wise in His seventh day creation of rest. Man was meant to take a break.

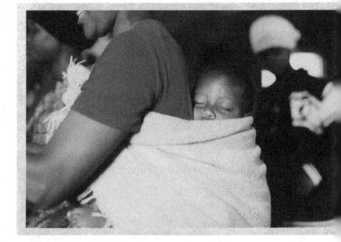

What interrupts the Sabbath? What rebellion against the natural order is there that can deny a gift that is so enjoyable? Usually it is our desire to get more money, more things, more prestige, more honor, more work, more accolades. It is the god of *more*.

Think about it. We take in all of creation and declare, "God, You are so good to give us such a beautiful gift!" We look at our children as they sleep secure in our homes and say, "Thank you, God, for these precious gifts and the wonderful home You have provided!" We come to church and speak blessings to God saying, "Lord! Thank you for the wonderful friends and Your gift of peace!"

But what do we do when it is time to rest from earthly pursuit and spend time with God? No time. Not now. Inconvenient. Not worth it.

We take the gift of God, created on the seventh day, and make a mockery of rest. We rebel against God and tell Him that His gift is not as valuable as our ability to get.

Take time to rest, dear friend. See it as what it is, the gift of God. God made man on the sixth day and on the seventh told him to rest. Adam's first full day alive was spent resting with God. In God's world, Sabbath was the first order of business for man.

And maybe that needs to be our perspective, too.

Family Time

Selah

Make a special effort today to just "be" with one another. Turn off all electronics. Set aside the list of things to do and enjoy each other's company. Do things that promote relationship:

- Play together.

- Take a short road trip.

- Get ice cream/coffee.

- Enjoy a meal together...at the table.

During your time together, be sure to talk! Talk about the positive parts of your day. Reminisce about the good times. Share about the things you're grateful for and the aspects of your family that you enjoy the most. Rest in the good and perfect gifts that come from the Father.

Open my eyes, Lord, not to Your blessings but to Your character. It is Your character that always loves me. When I see Your face, the trinkets of this world cease to catch my eye. Today, Lord, open my eyes to see you!

Day Nine

"And the Lord said to Moses, "How long do you refuse to keep My command and My laws? See! For the Lord has given you the Sabbath; therefore He gives you on the sixth day bread for two days. Let every man remain in his place; let no man go out of his place on the seventh day." (Exo. 16:28 NKJV)

They just didn't get it. God told them that He would provide a better life than they had in Egypt. In bondage, the Jews labored seven days under the harsh whip of the Egyptians. Under God's rule, the work week became one day less. On that day, the Sabbath, God's people were told to rest from every labor, including the daily task of gathering the manna that covered the desert like frost each night.

"Here is a gift," God says. "I will provide for you on the seventh day. I will feed you and protect you. I will give you a rest. I will multiply your work on the sixth day and it will be as valuable as two days labor. Enjoy! I have given you the Sabbath."

It was strictly a matter of faith. Would the people believe that God was able to provide for them better than they could for themselves? Some Jews answered with a resounding "No!" They went out and tried to work anyway. Just to see if God would keep His word, I'm sure, but God was angry and hurt.

It is a matter of faith, you see. If God says He will provide then it becomes an issue of believing He is able. If God says here is a gift called rest, then it becomes an issue of faith to take the gift and use it. And even though the Jews didn't keep God's special Law, the idea of trusting God through rest had been around since Adam. And that means that it remains until now.

So why don't we trust God and take a Sabbath? Sometimes we just don't get it either.

Family Time

Selah

Find examples of promotional prizes or giveaways. Show your children how the "free" gifts that are advertised are rarely without strings attached. Talk about how important it is to read the fine print and be careful of gimmicks because many promotions cannot be trusted.

Contrast these gifts with the truly free gifts from our Heavenly Father. Explain that with God's offer, there are no strings attached. He's created us to need rest. He's provided a plan for us to get rest. It's our choice to trust Him and receive it. Talk with your family about how you will receive God's gift of rest. What will that look like in your family?

Father, today I receive Your rest as the great gift You promised it would be. I will rest in You and with You today, Lord. I will trust you, Lord, as You pour out Your blessings today, open my eyes to see Your glory!

Day Ten

"Remember the Sabbath…" *(Deut. 5:12 NASB)*

It was July in Texas many years ago; hot, slow, and non-productive and that was the way I was determined to keep it. The only active bodies around town were those youngsters who never stop. You know them. They zip around on bikes all day long, laughing and yelling, red faces and shirtless backs glistening with sweat, caps turned backwards denying the good use of a hat altogether, and full of spit and vinegar. Summer is one long day to those boys and they were determined to make good use of every second. I had one of those. In the summer he insisted on a buzz haircut and had to be forced to wear shoes and a shirt. The trouble was he needed a dad to do things with and that was me.

"Remember the Sabbath," God spoke through Moses. Sabbath is a time for memorable things to be done. It is a time when the tempo changes and life is slowed to an observers pace. Like a giant parade, it is to pass with grandeur and pomp. A Sabbath is to be a remembered time.

So one day I left the cool of my office determined to enter the world of my son. I picked up the rowboat and told Joseph we were going fishing. We rowed up to the Falls and caught river critters in a screen for bait. Barefooted and bare-backed, and our hats crazy on our heads, life for a short time was about cool river water and a kid too soon to be grown and gone. All he wanted was me. My attention. My encouragement. Leave my world and enter into his.

"Laugh Dad. That is what my world is all about. Just take time to have fun with me." We pulled perch from the river and floated oh so lazily down the Guadalupe. And when our time was up, a Sabbath had been made, a memory forged. God took care of the business of life just like He said He would. Imagine that.

In the years to come, Joseph would find himself fretting about the big business of life too. And maybe someday, because I made a memory with him with a short Sabbath, he will choose his children over mammon too. *"Surely I have calmed and quieted my soul, like a weaned child with his mother is my soul within me. Oh, Israel, hope in the Lord (Psalm 131:2 NKJV)."*

19

Family Time

Selah

Get out the family calendar and plan a day of fun for each child. Set a budget, make a list and then plan a day when each child of the family has the undivided attention of one parent. It doesn't have to be elaborate. It doesn't have to be costly. Just plan a time when you can make a memory with each child. Do something your child wants to do. Enter his/her world, quiet your soul and enjoy the gift that the Lord has given you!

Father, as You sabbath with me, teach me to do the same with others. Show me how to rest so that the children around me will learn the same. You care for me, Lord! Teach me to care for others the same.

Day Eleven

"Remember the Sabbath day, to keep it holy." (Exo. 20:8 NKJV)

Do you remember when Sunday was the day that everyone prepared for? All the stores were closed and everything had to be purchased before the day. If you were missing an ingredient for your Sunday meal, you borrowed it from a neighbor. You couldn't run down to the corner market and pick it up because everything was closed. People, shop owners included, were not obliged to buy and sell.

There was an excitement in society when all that changed. First came the grocery stores who opened wide their doors to shoppers. We called it "convenient" and smiled as we padded the isles for this and that. No matter that the "Blue Laws" kept you from buying certain items. It was one more step for modern society.

But then a shift took place. More and more stores stayed open. Convenience was replaced with the selfishness of want. "I want to go to the store" or "I want to go shopping" became the reason for more and more to stay open.

And now? Now every store is open, including the local hardware store so you can fix that faucet between the golf game and mowing the lawn. "New Sunday Hours!" announces that we have finally been successful at making Sunday like every other day of the week.

In our pursuit of things and convenience, we have lost the virtue that kept the day set apart and holy.

- Things like uninterrupted time with our family and friends.

- The quietness of a community that is resting from the business of labor.

- The security of knowing that all are taking time to breathe easy and therefore it is okay.

But there is no going back. Maybe it is time to go forward and make the Sabbath holy with new traditions. Teaching our children that it is a special day and living our lives apart from the business of commerce could be a good start. And let's do it without a strangling sense of legalism. Now that would be refreshing.

This Saturday, prepare for Sunday. Not with just food or activities, but prepare the heart of your family for a time together and quietness and security.

Sunday could become Sabbath for us again.

Family Time

Selah

Take this moment to talk with your children about a new or renewed tradition that could make Sunday's special. This tradition needs to be relationship-centered. It needs to prompt increased connection with God and one another. Brainstorm some ideas that could remind everyone that the Sabbath is special and we are commanded to keep it holy. Talk about specifics. Plan the date when you will start your new tradition.

Here's an idea to get you started:

A special Sunday dinner where everyone eats heart pancakes to remembers the great love that God has lavished on each of us.

Lord, over and over You have committed to care for me, help me in my unbelief! I struggle, Lord, to do the very things You promised You would do. Today, I want to trust You and Your promises. Send Your Holy Spirit to convict me to trust You today.

Day Twelve

"Give us day by day our daily bread." (Luke 11:3 KJV)

It is easy to Sabbath on the Lord's Day. I am home on that day and in my element. People are nice and attentive. There is worship and sacrament, prayers and preaching. There is tradition and no one kicks too hard against the current.

But now it is the weekday and the week belongs to the world system, or so I've been told. The hurry-up world demands that we keep our silly tradition in its place. It is not time to rest, it is time to commerce. "Get out of your anemic world of religion and get on with life," they shout.

But I think of Adam and smile.

Adam was brand new to the earth and told to rest. All of creation before him to discover and rejoice in, but first, God says, "Take it all in with Me. Sit here awhile and Sabbath with Me."

So who are you going to listen to? The world or God? Yes, I know it is a workday and there are a million and one things to do, do, do. But is He Lord of the Sabbath, or is He Lord of All?

Do something to challenge the world system. Take time to sit with God. In the midst of the mess of mammon and striving after wind, ask God to come and Sabbath with you awhile.

Family Time

Selah

Do something simple today. Go outside with your family and pray (if the weather isn't conducive to going outside, find a video or photos through the Internet that reveal God's creation). Ask God to help you marvel at His creation – taking it all in. Invite Him to help you rest in and appreciate all that He has given. After you've prayed, watch and listen. Let God renew your gratitude for how He provides. Let God revive your joy at His creativity and splendor.

Today I choose to rest with you, Lord. I know that this is the Sabbath and I've been doing this for awhile now, but I need to continue to commit to Your Sabbath. I need to sit with You and be still. Thank You, Father, that You choose to do the same with me.

Day Thirteen

"It is good to give thanks to the Lord, And to sing praises to Your name, O Most High; to declare your loving kindness in the morning, and your faithfulness every night, on an instrument of ten strings, on the lute and on the harp, For You, Lord, have made me glad of Your work; I will triumph in the works of Your hands." (Psalm 92:1-4 NKJV)

What did the Jewish people do on the Sabbath? Don't think for a moment that they went through the day sullen-faced, wishing the day would end. Instead, they found their way to the synagogues that were in every village throughout Israel. On Sabbath feast days, such as Passover or the Feast of Trumpets, the Jewish nation would gather from around the world in Jerusalem and congregate, tens of thousands strong, at the Temple.

It was a time of great joy! The musicians would lead the people in the rousing songs of Zion! The people would dance, sing, eat, play and dance again as they sought to rejoice in the Sabbath of the Lord. The time was never spent in passive aloneness. Wherever God's people gathered, there was music, dancing, and joy!

Sound familiar? The Church of Jesus Christ takes the cue from the Psalms as to how we are to celebrate the Sabbath.

First, we are to gather together. There are plenty of times to be alone with God. Your prayer closet is one. Personal retreat times are another. But on the Lord's Day, the Christian's Sabbath, it is time to be in the House of the Lord. That means with the family of God.

Next, we are to sing. Make a joyful noise to the Lord! Don't be bashful as if someone is going to chastise you if you can't sing as well as another. Beautiful voices often come from cold hearts. God does not care how you sound for the only sound He listens for is a heart that beats passionately for Him.

Come and rejoice in God's Sabbath. Come with a desire to make a joyful noise and stop worrying about how you sound.

It could be just the ticket to put a song back in your heart.

Family Time

Selah

Take time on this day to enjoy music that celebrates our God. Play a favorite CD and sing along as a family. If someone in the family plays a musical instrument, sing some praise songs together. If there's a variety of taste in music, let every child/teen play his or her favorite Christian song or video for the rest of the family. Be sure to talk about why you like the music and why the lyrics are meaningful to you. Let this be a time to celebrate or discover the works of Jesus.

Lord, would you teach me to rejoice again? Would you teach me to find joy in the simple lessons You want to show me today? Thank you, Father, for Your divine rest today. I choose to rejoice in You!

Day Fourteen

But You, Lord, are on high forevermore. For behold, Your enemies, O Lord, For behold, Your enemies shall perish; All the workers of iniquity shall be scattered." (Psalm 92:8-9 NKJV)

There is a lot of talk about spiritual warfare these days, enough to make some people afraid. There is so much talk about hellish creatures in fact, that we forget that Jesus has already won the battle.

Sabbath reminds us that God has won. That He is on the throne. That He prevails over the forces of darkness and sin. "Hallelujah," Sabbath declares, "Jesus has won the victory!"

Paul the Apostle said it this way, *"Having disarmed principalities and powers, He made a public spectacle of them, triumphing over them in it (Col. 2:15 NKJV)."*

The picture he paints is one of a Conquering King who parades the defeated army, naked and ashamed, through the streets of the conquered land. With great pomp and celebration, the Conquering King shows the people of the land that they are no longer to fear the oppressing army. All of the people are in the streets to witness the public humiliation of the enemy. It is a grand day for the liberated people! It is a day when Rest returns to the land.

And that is what we do on the Sabbath. With joy and celebration we witness our Conquering King parade the disposed ruler of this world before us. He is a defeated foe, a beaten and enslaved nag of a being. There is no longer any reason to fear for our King reigns!

Don't miss your cue when the King comes by. Don't be found hiding from the defeated enemy or distracted from the celebration. Sabbath is the reminder that Jesus has indeed won the victory!

Rise up and rejoice! The King of the Sabbath reigns!

Family Time

Selah

Ask each family member to tell about their favorite villain in a story or movie. Do they most like the story of the Snow White and the character of the wicked witch? Are they most intrigued by Darth Vader or Superman's nemesis, Lex Luther? Discuss your interest and curiosity with these characters.

Next, talk to your family about our spiritual enemies. With age-appropriate terms, discuss how Satan has temporary power in this world, but there will come a day when he will be completely defeated. Finally, express your gratitude for how God is stronger than any enemy. He is ultimately more powerful than anything that might hurt us or cause us harm. "I'm so grateful that our God is stronger than *(blank)* that gives me great peace about *(blank)*."

King Jesus, I submit to You and You alone this day. I thank You that You have won the victory. Today I choose to walk in Your great grace. Fill me, Lord, with the thoughts of Your Kingdom reign.

Day Fifteen

*"O Lord, how great are Your works! Your thoughts are very deep.
A senseless man does not know, nor does a fool understand this." (Psalm 92:5-6 NKJV)*

Do you wonder?

Do you sometimes sit and wonder at the awesomeness of God and His creation? Do you look at the clouds on a summer day and wonder if heaven will be filled with clouds to play on? Do you listen to the thunder and wonder how God makes the sound so loud and fierce? Do you watch your child sleep and wonder what God will do with that young life? Do you wonder if dogs go to heaven? Do you wonder about all the people who have never heard of Christ? Do you wonder what streets of gold will really look like? Do you wonder if Jesus will look like the pictures that we draw and paint of Him? Do you wonder if God really knows your name—and if He does, how He remembers it? Do you wonder when Jesus will return? Do you wonder just how many hairs are on your head? Do you wonder how many stars are in the sky?

Wonders are part of Sabbath. Wonder, you see, is not blame.

"I wonder why He did this to me?" It is questioning, "What now, God?"

It is not mental exercise—"I need to figure this out." It is the knowing that God is more merciful, more loving, more concerned, more creative, more powerful, more intently drawn to detail than I and allowing the knowing to explode in absolute amazement.

He is a wonderful God!

"His name will be called Wonderful..." (Isa. 9:6 NKJV)

He does wonderful works!

"Many, O Lord my God, are Your wonderful works which you have done." (Psalm 40:5 NKJV)

When we take time to be captivated by wonder, the seed of wisdom is planted in our heart. When God does not have to always explain Himself, He bypasses our ways to show us things His way. Wisdom is birthed in wonderment. It is a mystery, a divine secret. Another thing that causes us to say, "I wonder how He does that?"

Family Time

Selah

Let this be a time when you wonder out loud with your family. If you could ask God about anything in the world, what would you ask? This isn't the time for mental exercises or figuring things out, but one of curiosity and amazement. How would you finish this sentence:

God, I was wondering *(blank)*.

Examples:

- God, I was wondering about fire ants. Couldn't you make them tickle instead of sting?

- God, I was wondering how you made the sky the perfect color blue?

- God, I was wondering how you thought up all those crazy-looking animals?

Open my eyes, Lord, to the wonder of Your creation. I need Your touch to see again, Holy One. Lord of the Sabbath, heal me and let me see!

Day Sixteen

"I have been anointed with fresh oil." (Psalm 92:10 NKJV)

Recipe for anointing oil... (Exo. 30:23-25 NKJV)

- Five hundred shekels of liquid myrrh (the spice of death)

- Half as much sweet-smelling cinnamon (the spice of flavor)

- Two hundred and fifty shekels of sweet-smelling cane (the spice of authority)

- Five hundred shekels of cassia (the spice of worship)

- One hin of olive oil (the symbol of the Holy Spirit)

Would you like a fresh anointing of the Holy Spirit? God commanded Moses and Aaron to mix a special blend of spices for anointing oil. The spices were purified until only the essence was left and then they were infused into the olive oil and strained leaving only the sweetness of their aroma behind.

It was an anointing that included death to self, symbolized by the myrrh that was used in embalming. If one submits to the anointing of God, it means death to one's own agenda.

Pure cinnamon was added which symbolized the unique flavor or gifting that each person anointed would bring to the community. The unique aroma of gifting pleases everyone as it is used to flavor life.

Cane was the spice of authority. It is interesting that the cane needed first to be bruised before it would emit the sweet odor it was known for. In other words, God's authority is best used by those not concerned about being bruised.

Cassia was the spice of worship. Taken from the Hebrew word which means to bend the body or neck in deference, it is the same word that the Hebrews used for worship. Those anointed by God must first be worshipers of God.

Olive oil was the most common, yet precious, commodity of Jewish life and served as the metaphor for the Holy Spirit. All the spices were mixed into this staple of life. Remember that the Holy Spirit is to be our staple of life from which all uniqueness flows.

The Book of Acts records that *"the disciples were first called Christians in Antioch."* The name means followers of the Anointed One. To receive the anointing of God you must commit to spending time with the Anointed One.

And Sabbath is the time to do just that. Spend time with the Anointed One. Spend time with the Lord of the Sabbath. He has a fresh anointing for you!

Family Time

Selah

Invite your family to participate in a test—a smell test. Bring several spices out of your spice cabinet and challenge family members to identify the spice and then tell if the spice "reminds" them of any particular event or memory. *(For example: Cinnamon might remind you of Thanksgiving and pumpkin pie. Rosemary might remind you of your favorite chicken dish and family dinners.)*

Next, remind everyone about the truth that God used fragrances in the Old Testament as reminders of relationship. He told the people of Israel to make certain perfumes/oils so that He would be reminded of a special relationship with the ones He loved, and so that His people would be reminded of the God who loved them. How does it make you feel to know that we have a God who WANTS to be reminded of His special relationship with you?

*Yes, Lord, I need Your anointing today. I ask
You that by the power of Your Holy Spirit
that You would fill me with the freshness of
Your grace. Pour out of my life Your life, Jesus.
Let Your anointing flow.*

Day Seventeen

"The righteous shall flourish like a palm tree, he shall grow like a cedar in Lebanon. Those who are planted in the house of the Lord shall flourish in the courts of our God." (Psalm 92:12-13 NKJV)

"He shall flourish... He shall grow... He shall flourish in the courts of our God," says the psalmist. "Shall" is a word that looks ahead. With great anticipation, "shall" declares that the future looks bright.

I have a friend who returned on furlough from a difficult assignment. After three years of intense struggle to establish a beachhead of righteousness in a pagan city, his spiritual vitality was drained. Though he still loved the country and the people that God has asked him to serve, he did not have any "shall" left in him. He was worn out, beyond hope, despairing of life and desperately in need of Sabbath.

An amazing thing takes place when we sabbath. Hope is restored. We begin to look ahead instead of behind. Our perspective begins to be God's again, instead of all the mistakes and failures of the past.

My friend is having his hope restored. With enough rest, he will begin to look forward to the work that awaits him in his adopted country. As he spends time with the Lord of the Sabbath, his heart will again look forward to the "shall" of God's plans.

But it takes wisdom to know when to stop, doesn't it? And once you have stopped, it takes faith to be quiet and rest. That is why God told us to sabbath on a weekly basis. Because we all need our hope restored.

Sabbath, you see, puts the "shall" back in our hearts.

Family Time

Selah

Take these moments to dream with your kids. Dream about what life might look like when they're "all grown up". Talk about the things that they/you are looking forward to in the years to come. Your dreams might start with: "I can't wait until *(blank),*" or "I'm looking forward to the time when *(blank),*" or "I am hoping for the time when *(blank).*" Close these discussions with a time of prayer. Thank God for how we can have hope because of Him and how He provides.

Today, Father, remind me of Your great promises. Though life is seldom what I want it to be, You are near. Thank you that Your plan is for a future and a hope. Thank you that Your plan is for me and not against me!

Day Eighteen

"He is my rock, and there is no unrighteousness in Him." (Psalm 92:15 NKJV)

Have you ever left church thinking, "That was well and good, but now it's time to get back to the real world?"

I thought a Sabbath gathering was the real world. The other world, the world of mammon and ego, is the counterfeit. It is the world that has been corrupted and that is the cardboard facade hiding the barrenness of the Fall.

The truth is that most people miss the whole point of Sabbath because they don't consider it real. But Sabbath is the ultimate statement that there is a better Kingdom than the kingdom of this world. On that day, as the rest of the world marches to the discord and destruction of commerce, mammon, and work, we declare, "Jehovah is the only one that will be forever. He is my rock and there is no unrighteousness in Him. He is immovable and wholly true to His word."

Is there any real value to the Sabbath? I guess that depends on which world is real.

Family Time

Selah

Show your family pictures of interesting rock formations, unusual caves or the Grand Canyon. Talk about the strength and fortitude of the rocks. Discuss the protection that rocks can provide and the security that they can give for hikers, climbers and travelers.

Next, talk about how God is compared to a rock. The psalmist finds rest, security and strength in God. Talk to your children about how God is a source of strength and security for you. "I know I can count on God because *(blank)*," or "I am confident about *(blank)* because God is *(blank)*," or "There was a time when I was scared/ uncertain, but God *(blank)*."

You said Your Kingdom was "not of this world." Lord, than I want to be more a part of Your Kingdom than this world. Today, I commit to Sabbath with You. Lord, show me Your ways.

Day Nineteen

*"Therefore, take no thought about tomorrow,
for tomorrow will take thought about the things of itself." (Matt. 6:34 MEV)*

Scene 1: "Going Away"

He didn't want his dad to leave for another trip. Dad was packing and puttering, ignoring the look the little boy was giving. Questions were coming fast from him. "Where are you going?" "When will you come home?" "How long is that?" "Why are you leaving?"

The man finally stopped. The little face was pensive the way a child's face was never meant to be.

"Joseph, do you need to tell Dad something? Is there something that is bothering you?" His emotions were screwed down tight, but anyone could tell that he was overloaded by his father leaving.

"Dad," he said, "If I fall, who will pick me up?" A desperate play or childlike honesty? I think the latter. Dad is the one who brings balance to his life. Dad is responsible to steady the course as we walk together. And his going left the little boy without his rudder, without his captain.

Scene 2: "A Place for You"

The disciples were perplexed. Jesus had just told them He was leaving. He was the captain of their souls, the sure keel of their lives.

"Where I am going you cannot come." Like little boys, the eleven screwed down their emotions tight. Now's not the time for tears. Now is the time to be men. But what is that glistening in the glow of the oil lamp? It must be sweat, surely Jesus couldn't be…Well, yes, it is a tear. The Master's crying. For us.

"I go to prepare a place for you. And I'll come back. Where I am, that is where you will be too." The tears flow. There is sadness, yet it is as if the very air they breath is thick with peace. How can all this be?

Epilogue:

Jesus prepares a place for us, and that place is in His Father's house. On that day when we see Him face to face, we will fully understand the Sabbath of the Lord. Until then there is striving to enter in, but on that day striving will be no more.

Tears will be wiped away. Sadness will be banished. The thorns of sin will be faint memories. And the hearts of little boys will never be perplexed again. I, for one, look forward to the eternal Sabbath that awaits the children of God. "Maranatha, O Lord, come!"

Family Time

Selah

Take a few moments to reminisce about the times when you have been physically separated from your family members and how you longed to be reunited. Tell stories that start with these words, "I remember really missing *(blank) (name your family member)* when *(blank)*. I couldn't wait to be together again because *(blank)*."

Next, reflect on the truth that this is the way that Jesus feels about us. He longs to be reunited with us. He really misses being (physically) with us and can't wait to be together. In fact, Jesus is in heaven right now, praying for us, talking to the Father about us and preparing a place for us to live in heaven alongside Him. How do you feel when you reflect on a God like that? Talk to one another about your gratitude and your joy. "I feel *(blank)* when I imagine that Jesus *(blank)*."

Sometimes, when life is hard, I think of Heaven and what it will be like. Lord, help me today to always keep Heaven as my goal and not gaining more of the trinkets of this world. Help me today to live so that someday I will finish well.

Day Twenty

"Take no thought about tomorrow…" (Matt. 6:34 MEV)

Scene 1: "Sweet Little Babies"

The two sweet little babies were playing happily, when one toy suddenly became the favorite. It wasn't anything special. Just another bit of something that had the distinct look of living on the bottom of the toy box. Previously overlooked in favor of more enticing treasures, the trinket was more toy box filler than anything else.

But now it was the crown jewel. Without hesitation, the two sweet little babies became screaming adversaries. The toy became the prize, and the battle cry became "Mine!" "Mine!" "Mine!"

Scene 2: "The Auction Block"

You could tell who the family members were. They were huddled in an emotionally charged semi-circle at the back of the crowd. It would remind you of animals protecting their young from hungry wolves in winter. The gavel smacked down time and again as their life, and that of the generations before, passed over the auction block.

Now the house, their home, was next. Ten minutes and it was over. The auctioneer wasn't being spiteful, but he could have been more careful. He looked at the buyer and said "When will you take possession?"

Take. Whenever someone takes, someone else loses what was once theirs.

Epilogue:

The babies took from one another.

The buyer took possession.

It's not an evil word but it is certainly aggressive. The consonants crackle to life with a descriptive explosive sound. *"Take."* Aggressive, isn't it?

And Jesus said, *"Take no thought."*

It's like He knew our lower nature would grapple for the prize. Our desire for all would move us to take possession for ourselves. He knew that. So He said "Do not. Do not take."

Just let it be. Don't wrestle with God over the struggles of life. Sabbath means to rest. And that means there is no taking allowed.

Family Time

Selah

Explain to your family that sometimes God's way of life can seem so opposite of our ways. We think it's best to be first, but God says it's best to be last. We think it's better to receive, God says it's best to give. Talk about how your family would be different if everyone in the family only "took" from one another, no one in the family "gave".

Next, help your children reflect on all the ways that God gives to us first. He took initiative to give us salvation, forgiveness, grace, mercy, compassion, and life! Express your gratefulness to God. "God, thank You for giving me *(blank)*. I am so grateful because *(blank)*. Please help me concentrate on giving more to others in my family."

Lord, I am too often taking back what I have first given to You. I am often fearful that if I do not take control then I will lose what I am striving for. Would You visit me with Your Peace today, Lord? I know Your peace is what I need.

Day Twenty-One

"Take no thought about tomorrow..." (Matt. 6:34 MEV)

Have you ever had a troubling thought rob you of a minute, an hour, or a day? Like a thief, it cases out your life, looking for the open window, the unguarded door to your heart.

All of a sudden, or so you would be led to believe, you have been robbed, mugged, violated by Worry. Without a guard to challenge the intruder, the incessant robber dressed in the disguise of an innocent thought violates our heart home and steals us blind.

But God promised us a great security system. Philippians 4:7 (ASV) says this, *"And the peace of God, which passeth all understanding, shall guard your hearts and your thoughts in Christ Jesus."*

Sabbath includes peace. And when we enter God's rest, His Sabbath, then God's peace will stand sentry against the robber of worrisome thought. There is no reason to lose a minute, let alone an hour or a day, to the thief named Worry.

I guess you could say that with Sabbath comes God's peace officer who will stand guard at the door of your heart.

So let Sabbath arm you against a break-in. God's security system of peace is a powerful presence against the robber of worry.

Family Time

Selah

Talk about the security measures that help keep your home safe. It may be an actual alarm system monitored by a third party, or it could be the set of locks on your doors and windows. Remind your family that God's peace is like a security system for our lives. His peace is what helps keep us safe from worry. Here's how that works. One Peter 5:7 (NASB) says that we can be free from worry (have peace) when we remember that He cares for us. Next, tell stories about the amazing ways God has cared for your family. Remind one another of God's care in the past, so you can rest in His security today. "We can rest in God's care for our family because He's the kind of God who *(blank)*."

If it is one thing that will interrupt my Sabbath it is worry, Lord. So right now, I choose to cast all my cares on You. Thank you, Lord, that You promised to bear my burdens. I love you today, Lord of the Sabbath.

Day Twenty-Two

"Take no thought about tomorrow…" (Matt. 6:34 MEV)

Conventional wisdom says that tomorrow is "a better day."

"There is always tomorrow."

"Tomorrow is another day."

"Look to tomorrow."

Tomorrow is portrayed as always having a cool breeze and a smile to boot. Unless you live in the real world, that is. That is where the troubles of today are compounded by the thought of tomorrow. I don't know about you, but that is where I pitch my tent sometimes.

The Bible's prescription for worry is simple. Worry could be defined as fear of the future. In other words, worry is living in the unknown of what we think tomorrow will bring. When life is stressful, others try to encourage us to "look to the future" but for some, looking to the future torments us with fear because the future is always an unknown. That is why Jesus said, "Don't worry. Don't live in fear of tomorrow."

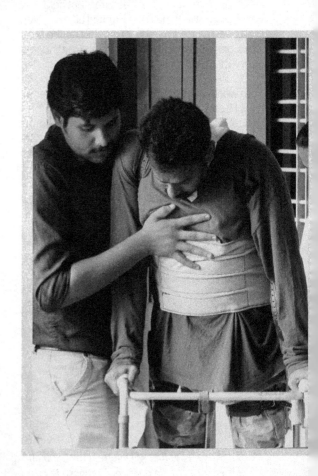

He instructs us to live in the struggles of now. Not to get caught up in yesterday's hurts—which produces anger. Do not dwell on what could be tomorrow—which produces fear. Live fully in today. That is where Jesus promises to walk with us and where He promises to meet our needs.

Do not look to tomorrow or you will be looking in the wrong place for Sabbath. Instead, commit the struggles of today to your yoke-mate, Jesus. Tomorrow, after all, is an excessively heavy burden to bear. Especially when it is still today.

Family Time

Selah

Make today your opportunity to "be fully present" with your children and family. As you're having dinner today or hanging around the house together, challenge your family members to notice the little things about one another. Do your best listening. Do your best observing of one another. Don't worry about plans or events for tomorrow. Set aside things to do and tasks to accomplish. For a few moments on this day, notice the twinkle of your children's eyes. Listen to the joy in the voices that surround you. Revel in the moment. Celebrate being together. Find gratitude in today. "I heard/saw something special in our family today. I noticed/heard *(blank)*."

Lord, I admit that tomorrow is one of those things most difficult to not think about. So today I ask you to show me Your goodness and mercy. Let me be so captured by Your good care that tomorrow will fade from my thoughts.

Day Twenty-Three

"I did not come to bring peace but a sword." (Matt. 10:34 NIV)

Now walk with me on this one. Be ever so patient and see with the eyes of your soul and please don't rush ahead. I want to walk around this scripture, and see the Sabbath. In the violence of forceful intrusion, I want to turn and discover the rest of God.

Jesus was more than an irritant to the Pharisees. His whole mission was to destroy and conquer the world of legalism and empty religiosity with Rest. His methods made their white-washed souls crawl in their rich robes, like worms through rotted fruit. They would have much preferred if He had assembled an army of renegade Jews and attacked the Temple. There was nothing more violent to their little world of decayed legalism than the life of Sabbath that He offered to "whosoever would come."

His methods were backwards from every other conquering king.

- He attacked the citadels of pride with humility.

- His weapons were those of holy guerrilla warfare.. subversive and innocent looking.

- Violence through acts of peace.

- Destruction through an extended hand of non-violence.

We are invited to do the same. When we take God's rest, we conquer the chaotic world that is desperately running to keep up with itself. Like Jesus, we enter into the world yet refuse to submit to the worlds rules.

Where there is turmoil, Sabbath demands peace. Where there is chaos, Sabbath explodes on the scene with restful order. Where there is stressful heartache, Sabbath takes control with comfort. The kingdom of the world never sees what is coming. It is accustomed to dealing in terms of strength and Sabbath simply does not look very strong.

Sabbath is God's sucker punch.

Before you can tap into the power of the Sabbath, you will have to spend time with God. You will have to still your soul in order to enter into the war room of Sabbath rest.

"In quietness and confidence shall be your strength (Isa. 30:15 NASB)."

Conquering this world system, you see, takes a mighty quiet soul.

Family Time

Selah

Isaiah 30:15 reminds us that strong families look for ways to increase the "quiet" in their lives. Spend the next few minutes talking about the ways in which you might bring more peace to your home. Reassure the kids that this doesn't necessarily mean our homes need to look more like school. It could mean: finding ways to cut down on the busyness of life, fewer sporting events, fewer things to do, less yelling and more patience, less name calling and more respect, less criticism and more praise. Invite everyone in the family to participate in the discussion. Your ideas might sound like these: "I think our home could be more peaceful if we (blank)." "I think our family could have more calm, if we had less (blank) and more (blank). Here's what I could do to help make that happen (blank)."

Help me to be quiet today, Lord. While the world and all its troubles scream for my attention, help me to quiet my soul and listen to Your voice.

Day Twenty-Four

In 1995, I was caught in one of the worst snow storms that New York City had ever witnessed. All day long I could do nothing except watch the constant news reports about the tremendous blizzard that was dumping foot after foot of snow on the city.

New York fought a good fight but around mid-morning it was apparent that the city had lost the battle of business as usual. The city officials closed the city down. Streets were closed to traffic. Kids were sent home from schools. Stores shut their doors and sent employees into the elements. Only the necessary happened.

An amazing thing took place. People began to talk to one another. They stopped on the street and conversed. Neighbors who never spoke were laughing together and playing in the snow. Hard-bitten New York became neighborly all because of a snow storm. Forced to slow down and stop, the city lost its identity of unfriendliness and became "small town" for a day.

Amazing.

No telling what would happen if the city decided to do that on its own. Shutting down for a day each week might just change the personality all week long. Maybe God knew what He was doing when He commanded us to do the same.

Jesus said, "Come unto Me all you who are heavy laden and I will give you rest." It is an invitation to participate in Sabbath, the rest of the Lord. Too many people wait until a storm forces a Sabbath shut-down before they respond. Don't get caught like that.

Take your Sabbath. It's the one sure way that Jesus teaches us to rest.

Family Time

Selah

Talk as a family how animals were trained in the days of Jesus. The younger animal was placed in a yoke with an older, more experienced animal. When the farmer was ready to work, he would rely on the experienced animal to show the younger how to accomplish the work. Jesus is our More Experienced Guide. Talk to your family about the ways that you need Jesus' help and guidance. With His gentle and loving guidance, we can experience more rest in our family. Begin your sharing with words like: "I want Jesus's help me know how to *(blank)*. I am grateful He is a gentle and kind Teacher because *(blank)*."

I embrace Your Sabbath today, Lord. I embrace Your rest and desire to carry Your rest to troubled souls. Open my eyes and let me see others the way You do.

Day Twenty-Five

"Martha, Martha, you are worried and troubled about many things." (Luke 10:41 NKJV)

   Martha and Mary were sisters who lived in a suburb of Jerusalem called Bethany. Fully devoted to Jesus, both sisters are noted for their service and affection. This story tells of an important lesson learned on one of Jesus' visits.

   Jesus and His disciples were always glad to come to Bethany, the home of Mary and Martha. Their home was full of joy and laughter, much more pleasant than the constant arguments of the Pharisees. This visit was no different. Having been graciously received into Martha and Mary's home, the disciples felt loved by these special friends of Jesus.

   There was much to do in those days when you invited guests to dinner. In ancient Israel, a guest was treated with the utmost honor and it was a disgrace to not be well prepared. Martha and Mary had been trained by their mother's example in how to receive guests into their home. Some of the things that would be necessary are:

- A special servant at the front door to wash the feet of the guests. This was necessary because of the dusty roads and sandals that everyone wore.

- Another servant to offer the guests sweet smelling oil for their hair. It was a special treat to the weary traveler to be offered this gift of oil and spices.

- Food and drink galore! Do you remember the story of the Wedding at Cana? Had Jesus not stepped in and provided miraculous wine, the family giving the wedding would have been disgraced in their village.

   Martha was worried with all the many details and quickly became agitated with her sister who was more interested in hearing the wonderful things that Jesus was saying. Finally, she could take no more.

   "Lord, have you noticed that I have been left to prepare everything by myself while my sister sits and listens to you? Please tell her to help me!" she said.

   Jesus was kind, but always truthful. He recognized that Mary had chosen between impressing the many guests with wonderful hospitality and simply spending time with Him.

   "Martha, Martha," He said ever so gently. "You are worried about so many things. But one thing is really needed. And Mary has chosen that good part, which will not be taken away from her."

   Years from now, no one will remember the impressive dinner parties, wonderful speeches, or athletic prowess that seem so important now. All of the memories of those times will fade like an old photograph in a shoe box. What will not be taken from us are the lessons that we learn as we spend time with Jesus. What will not be taken away are the times that we chose to spend with Him, even when others think there are more important things to be done.

Family Time

Selah

Jesus loved to make special trips to Bethany so that He could spend time with Mary, Martha and Lazarus. In fact, Jesus went out of His way to visit their home; they were like family for Him. We have an incredible privilege. Jesus wants to have this same kind of relationship with us. He wants us to be His Bethany. Isn't it amazing that Jesus wants to visit with us? Isn't it incredible that the Savior wants to spend "family time" with us? Talk about how you feel about this truth.

"I feel *(blank)* when I remember that Jesus wants to spend "family time" with me."

Thank you for the life of these two saints,
Lord. Thank you for sharing their story and
reminding me to spend time with You instead
of all of the pressing and good chores that can
rob my time and focus. Today I choose to sit at
Your feet as often as possible.
Thank you for Sabbath!

Day Twenty-Six

"Be still and know that I am God." (Psalm 46:10 NKJV)

I have a revelation for you. It is not a big one like a vision of heaven or anything. It is not dramatic or sensational or even awe inspiring. But it has changed my life and that is why I have decided to share it with you. Here it is.

God's world is backwards from mine. His time runs counterclockwise. While my world is bright and glaring and gaudy, His world is best seen in the darkroom of silence and meditation. My world is loud and chaotic. In His world, He speaks softly in peace and quiet. In my world only the strong survive. In His world those who are weak are strong, those who are blessed are poor, and those who are hungry are filled.

Jesus looked a strong man in the eye one day and said, *"My kingdom is not of this world (John 18:36 NASB)."* Why do I spend so much energy trying to convince Him that His Kingdom should be of this world? I insist on the comforts of society. I worry about the food, the drink, the clothes on my back. It seems that sooner or later I would understand that my love for this world is what keeps me from entering into His. Like a camel overloaded with riches and treasures, I can't squeeze through the passage way into His kingdom.

In John 14:3 (NASB), He said it this way to His friends, "I go to prepare a place for you." They didn't like that. They wanted Him to stay and make a place in our world. They would have much preferred, at least at that moment in time, to not have to face the fact that in order to enter into His Kingdom, we must leave our kingdom behind.

His Kingdom is so unlike ours. His Kingdom could not be more different. Despite the fascination I hold for this world's kingdom, my heart yearns for His peace, the peace that passes all understanding. My heart yearns for His fellowship, that kind of fellowship that reaches deep and declares, "It is well with my soul." And in order to find that, I must unload and come empty as a poor man. I must come with tears as one who mourns. I must be meek, humbled, that I might have authority. I must be hungry and thirsty for righteousness, merciful and pure in heart if I am to catch a glimpse of God. And peace-making must be my passion that I might gain a throne as God's son.

You see what I mean? His world is backwards from mine. And that is why I must sabbath with Him. Because when I still and quiet my soul, when I slow down and stop long enough to listen, He spins me in the right direction. And that is when I understand that maybe it is my world that runs counter to His.

In other words, it is me that runs backwards, not Him.

Family Time

Selah

This day is a great day for an object lesson. Drive your children to an empty parking lot (Or if you have teens, you might let them behind the wheel). Tell your family that you will be driving from one point in the parking lot to another point in the lot. Drive from Point A to Point B (adding a few obstacles, just to make it interesting). Next, tell the kids that you're going to drive the same route, but this time you'll be driving backwards. Drive from Point A to Point B, making a few intentional driving errors along the way. Discuss with your family: Which way was the better way? Which way got us there more safely and more successfully?

Explain that God's way is the best way. We sometimes think that we know best, but unless we match up with God's plan, it's like we're driving backwards. His plans, His ideas, and His ways of living provide more safety and are ultimately more successful.

Lord, give me a clear glimpse of Your Kingdom today! Let me see the difference in this world and Your Kingdom. I choose to go Your direction and not the world's, Lord.

Day Twenty-Seven

*"For it pleased the Father...by Him to reconcile all things to Himself
...having made peace through the blood of His cross." (Col. 1:19-20 NKJV)*

Do you know what the biggest deception of peace is? Religion.

That's right. To attain holiness by works apart from the miraculous work of God's Spirit is the grand deceiver of them all. Religion forces us to work for peace with God. Religion constantly goes back to the table to discuss one or more minute details of the Writ of Reconciliation between us and God. And the biggest deception is we think God remains interested in our vain attempts to reconcile on our terms.

What does it mean to reconcile? It means to make peace, to cease hostilities, to go beyond cease fire and on to joy in the streets. To reconcile means that someone has won the war, the conflict is resolved, and a close relationship is reestablished.

Reconciliation is very rare. Most often, what is established is a counterfeit peace that is nothing more than a leaky dam storing a flood of hatred for the future. In fact, there is only one real reconciliation that has ever taken place. All others have been partial at best.

Shadows of true reconciliation.

Charlatans of resolve.

Cruel fakery in the guise of joy.

Sin's work was complete and total. All creation was at odds with God. But the war ended at the cross when Jesus wrote the terms of reconciliation with His own blood. He, Jesus, is our Peace and he has broken down every wall that separated us from God.

The ceasing of hostilities means that peace returns to the land. And with peace, harmony with God. And with harmony, rest for the citizens of the land. Because of the one true reconciliation in history, you and I can cease from the labor intensive activity of a false peace.

So take your ease, Citizen. You have been reconciled to the Lord of the Sabbath.

Family Time

Selah

Talk about this custom: When two people have had a disagreement, we sometimes ask them to seal the terms of their new agreement, by shaking hands. "Shaking on it" represents that the conflict has been resolved, the issue decided.

Because of our sin, we have conflict with God. He desperately wants to be our friend, but because He is holy, He cannot be a part of sin. Here's the truth we can rest in: When Jesus died on the cross, He is the one who helped us resolve our conflict with God. It's because of Jesus, that we can "shake hands with God." The issue is decided. Shake hands with your family and celebrate this truth: "I'm so grateful that Jesus made it possible to have a friendship with God."

I rest in Your everlasting arms today, Father. I thank you that my account of hostilities against the Kingdom has been settled by the blood of Your Son. Open my heart today so that I can live in peace with myself and others. Let Your Kingdom truths come true in my life today.

Day Twenty-Eight

"Let us build these cities and make walls around them, and towers, gates, and bars, while the land is yet before us, because we have sought the Lord our God; we have sought Him and He has given us rest on every side." (2 Chron. 14:7 NKJV)

Asa was a good king. The history that is written about him in the book of Chronicles records the great reforms that he made, and how his example brought Judah back to the worship of Jehovah.

In the first several verses of his three-chapter history, a recurring theme develops that enunciates his reign.

"...the land was quiet for ten years (2 Chron. 14:1 NKJV)."

"...the kingdom was quiet under him" (2 Chron. 14:5 NKJV)."

"...the land had rest (2 Chron. 14:6a NKJV);"

"...the Lord had given him rest (2 Chron. 14:6b NKJV)."

"...He (the Lord) has given us rest on every side (2 Chron. 14:7 NKJV)."

Quietness and rest were the hallmark of this man's reign because he sought to serve God with integrity. As a result of his active stance against idolatry and the immortality of the land, he discovered a long standing promise God had spoken to the children of Israel while they were still in the desert between Egypt and Canaan.

The promise was simple. "If you keep My commandments, I will bless you with the rest (Sabbath). If you do not keep My commandments, I will curse you with trouble." With simple obedience to the plan of God, Asa ushered into the whole of Israel rest.

But his response to God's blessing was unusual to say the least. When Asa recognized the Sabbath of the Lord, he instructed the people to build fortified cities complete with towers, gates, and bars. Instead of indulging the grace of God, he recognized the time of blessing to be an opportunity for great achievement, and it was a good thing, too.

Enter Serah the Ethiopian—a man with an evil mission. With an army of one million men and three hundred chariots, he planned to destroy Israel. His army is the largest army mentioned in the Old Testament and their defeat is the greatest military victory in Israel's history. And it took place at one of the most restful times of all. The lesson? Don't mistake God's rest as a time to let down your guard. Another king named David made that mistake and met a woman named Bathsheba.

The Sabbath of the Lord is a time to fortify your city, not to let down your guard. Strengthen the bonds of marriage, family, and church during this time. It is a sure defense against the attack of the enemy.

Family Time

Selah

God told the children of Israel that if they would keep His commandments, He would give them rest. Claim this same promise for your family. Think about some of the commands that God has for families. Could you benefit from keeping these commandments more often, so that you can look forward to more peace in your family? Discuss, make plans to live out and look for God's promise to come true!

- Only saying words that build up, rather than words that tear down (Eph. 4:29 NASB).

- Accepting one another's imperfections, quirks and differences (Rom. 15:7 NASB).

- Resolving conflict quickly, not leaving hurts unaddressed (Eph. 4:26 NASB).

Abba, thank you for the family of God! Thank you for the bonds of love and the ligaments of peace with which You have joined me to others. Today, I choose to walk in Your love and express it to those who You have loved me through. So often, I have asked You to open my eyes. Do it again today, Abba! Open my eyes to those you have so graciously joined my life to in Your Kingdom.

Day Twenty-Nine

"If because of the Sabbath, you turn your foot from doing your own pleasure on My holy day, and call the Sabbath a delight, the holy day of the Lord honorable and honor it, desisting from your own ways, from seeking your own pleasure and speaking your own word, then you will take delight in the Lord and I will make you ride on the heights of the earth; and I will feed you with the heritage of Jacob your father, for the mouth of the Lord has spoken." (Isa. 58:13-14 NASB)

The human heart resists the Sabbath of the Lord. Convinced that "I can do it all myself," mankind determines to breech the great gift of God and call it a curse…or legalism…or another man's religion. Worse are those who have convinced themselves that because Sabbath is an old testament construct that it has lost its significance and power.

Sabbath is about gaining God's promises, not keeping a rule. Over and over, He states that the return on the investment of time spent solely trusting Him will result in untold benefits.

I cringe when I hear someone who values work, pleasure, or time for self, over the deliberate act of Sabbath. That is to say, when someone "skips" church to gain time to themselves, all I can think of is, why are you robbing God? That's right. The Sabbath, like the tithe, belongs to the Lord. And there is no profit in robbing God of what belongs to Him.

There is great profit in giving God what He requests, especially when what He requests is a seed that will yield to my great benefit.

"*If* because of the Sabbath, you turn your foot away from doing your own pleasure…

If you call the Sabbath a delight…

If you honor it and take delight in the Lord…

Then I will make you ride on the heights of the earth, I will feed you with the heritage of Jacob (Isa. 58:13-14 NASB italics added)!"

The Sabbath is the key to many conditional promises, just like the tithe. Many progressive saints today are missing the whole point, and the blessing as a result. Sabbath is not a sacrifice, it is an act of faith. When I stop to be with the Lord and His people, He releases the blessings and the wisdom of heaven to me. It's simple, really. Too simple, it would seem, for such modern people like us.

Family Time

Talk today about the privilege you have to stop and be with the Lord – individually, as a family and with His church family. Share your gratitude for the accessibility of our God. Tell your family the reasons why you love corporate worship. Let your children and family hear your thanksgiving for the opportunity to be with the Lord and His people.

Lord, the war goes on between my flesh and Your Holy Spirit. But You, O Lord, are high and lifted up and to You and You only do I bow! I call Your Sabbath a delight today. I honor and delight in You today. Now Lord, feed me with the heritage of Heaven as You promised!

Selah

Day Thirty

Jesus went through the grain fields on the Sabbath, and His disciples became hungry and began to pick the heads of grain and eat. But when the Pharisees saw this, they said to Him, "Look, Your disciples do what is not lawful to do on a Sabbath." (Matt. 12:1-2 NASB)

Jesus is Lord. Lord of what? He is the Lord of the Sabbath. He is the Lord of Rest. Others attributed titles to Him like "Lord of all," "Lord of heaven and earth," and "Lord of glory," but Lord of the Sabbath is the only thing He claimed while here on the earth.

Jesus came for one purpose, and that was to buy back the sons and daughters of Adam and Eve. That single sacrifice began an avalanche of restoration power that preceded the cross with His ministry here on the earth. This was one of them. He was Lord of the Sabbath then, and remains Lord of the Sabbath today.

Only a few times does the Lord tell us about Himself. His humility was unwavering and He relied on behavior and action instead of constant self-disclosure. But one time He reveals a great truth about Himself. He said, *"Come unto Me, all ye that labor and are heavy laden, and I will give you rest...I am meek and lowly in heart: and ye shall find rest unto your souls (Matthew 11:28-30 KJV)."*

I do not understand the relation between being "meek and lowly" and the ability to give my soul rest. It is beyond my understanding, too difficult for me. But Jesus claimed not only the ability to bring me rest but the title of being the Lord, the Master, the Ruler of Rest. Before the great sacrifice was accomplished, He had already begun to release the blessings of His nature to "whosoever would come."

That is what He still brings. That is what He still desires for you. By naming Himself the Lord of the Sabbath, He revealed one of His greatest joys—He loves to bring you rest. He longs to be with you and bring you peaceful quiet. Can you, like Him, be meek enough and humble enough to receive that great gift?

He is Lord of heaven and earth, Lord of glory, Lord of all for sure. But right now, in the stress and fears of these times and season, I need Him to be my Ruler of Rest. How about you?

Family Time

Selah

Matthew 11 reminds us that Jesus is Lord, Guide and Giver of Rest. As a family, reflect on some of the ways in which you might need Jesus' guidance. Do you need Jesus to guide you in how to forgive one another, be patient with one another, kind to one another, more respectful of one another? Share your ideas: "I need Jesus to guide me in how to *(blank)*."

Next, because Jesus is Lord, He can certainly answer these requests. Pray together as a family. Ask Jesus for His help. And then because He is the Giver of Rest, look for the peace that He brings to your family.

Abba, I pray that You would do as Your word promised, "For with the Lord, there is lovingkindness and abundant redemption." Show me Your ways today, Lord. As I rest in You, show me Your paths.

Day Thirty-One

"You shall remember that you were a slave in the land of Egypt, and the Lord your God redeemed you; therefore I command you this thing today." (Exo. 20:8 NKJV)

Jesus instructed the disciples, *"...do this in remembrance of Me (1 Cor. 11:24 NKJV)."* He instructed us to remember because He knew the great potential we have to forget. Can you imagine forgetting the sacrifice of the cross? Can you imagine forgetting the trauma of the passion or the greater love that laid down His life for you? Like a love that grows cold from neglect, like a marriage that slowly finds the oneness of years separated by the cold wall of indifference, distraction will always result in a lapse of love. How sad that He would be compelled to say those words. At His final meal before execution, His cry was, "please don't forget Me."

Sabbath is to our deliverance what communion is to His sacrifice. God came to the Israelites and said not to forget that they were slaves whose only deliverance came at the direct hand of the Almighty. Remembering you were a slave was not the issue. Remembering that you're deliverance came from the direct intervention of the Mighty Jehovah God and not the self-made plans of men was the bone of contention. In other words, one day a week they were told to remember by allowing God to provide for them just like in the Exodus.

In the New Testament, Jesus borrows directly from the old and uses the word "remember." Over sixty times in the Old Testament and almost the same in the New, Sabbath is mentioned. Surely, if God chose to make it such a regular part of His people's history it meant more than just a day off to go to church.

"Remember the Sabbath"... "Do this to remember Me." The link between the two is not grounded in dead traditions. Deep in the heart of God He wants us to remember that:

- Jesus's sacrifice, represented by the cup and the bread, is our only hope to escape eternal punishment, He paid a debt I could not pay.

- Secondly, shutting out this world and its influences for a brief time to spend time with Him will remind me that He is God and I am not.

So, remember: The plans He has for you are for good and not evil. If you want to walk His paths, Sabbath points the way forward.

Family Time

Selah

Ask your children to think about how they've felt when they've been forgotten. Have they been forgotten when someone passed out cupcakes? Has anyone forgotten them when party invitations come around? When names are called or awards are given? "There was a time when someone forgot to *(blank)* and I felt *(blank)* because *(blank)*."

Next, talk about the pain that Jesus must feel when we forget about Him. Just like us, He wants to be remembered. He wants to be acknowledged. He wants to be included. It may be a little weird, but can you hurt for Jesus? Spend a few moments in prayer as a family. Tell Jesus about your heart for Him. Let Jesus know that above all, you want to remember Him.

Jesus, You promised to send Your Holy Spirit who would bring to remembrance all the things You said. Today, I invite the Holy Spirit to constantly remind me of Your Word and the promises You give in Your Sabbath. I love You, Lord. Please speak to me!

Day Thirty-Two

"Jesus went through the grain fields on the Sabbath, and His disciples became hungry and began to pick the heads of grain and eat. But when the Pharisees saw this, they said to Him, 'Look, Your disciples do what is not lawful to do on a Sabbath.'" (Matt. 12:1-2 NASB)

The disciples were hungry. Jesus did not have the means to feed them, and so passing through the field, they picked the grains and ate. The Pharisees wasted no time. Only a few months before, Jesus was the honored guest at their lavish banquets but now they were only there to criticize as the needs of the hungry were met. They criticized Jesus, not the disciples, by the way.

The protest was about rules, not the condition of man. It was about formalities and stoic methods of observance, not the hunger of those who were serving the Kingdom. Just like today when the law takes the heart of worship and replaces it with empty form, the keepers of the law made certain that the protest was loud and clear.

The Sabbath was the final straw that hatched the plot to kill Jesus. Not miracles, His teaching, doctrine or lifestyle. The Sabbath became the center of controversy because of one issue. That issue was control. Would God be in control and bring the children of Adam and Eve back to citizenship in His Kingdom, or would man control through forms of godliness while denying the power of their Creator?

This is the central issue in the heart of every person. Who will control? Will it be me or will it be God? Will it be my ability to look better, pray longer and quote more than someone else or will it be Jesus, meek and lowly of heart? Sometimes, breaking the laws of religion are the very acts of obedience to the King of Kings.

Family Time

Selah

Read the following verse with your family: *"For anyone who enters God's rest also rests from their works, just as God did from His." (Heb. 4:10 NIV)*

Remind everyone that sometimes we mistakenly believe that we have to earn our way to heaven or work our way into right relationship with God. This verse brings incredible relief. Use your words and experience to underscore this truth for your children: "I used to worry that I had to *(blank)* in order to get to heaven and become a part of God's family, but now I know that *(blank)*."

Save me from self-righteousness, Lord. Save me from pretending and show me the areas of control that I grip in my hand, fearful to give up. I give You control of my life, Lord. Mold me and make me Your vessel for Your service today.

Day Thirty-Three

"... listen attentively to Me...bring no load in through the gates of this city on the Sabbath day..." (Jer. 17:24 NASB)

"They tie up heavy burdens and lay them on men's shoulders, but they themselves are unwilling to move them with so much as a finger. But they do all their deeds to be noticed by men; for they broaden their phylacteries and lengthen the tassels of their garments. They love the place of honor at banquets and the chief seats in the synagogues, and respectful greetings in the market places, and being called Rabbi by men (Matt. 23:4-7 NASB)." Jesus was talking about religious leaders, those who were charged with demonstrating a relationship with God. They wore the right clothes, ate the right food, used the proper language, and hung around with the right crowd. The problem was that everyone else had jobs, families, and food to put on the table, so all of the rules became impossible to keep.

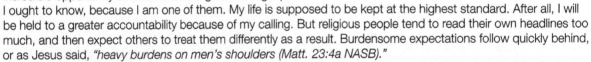

In today's church, there are those who have the incredible opportunity to make their living from the gospel. I ought to know, because I am one of them. My life is supposed to be kept at the highest standard. After all, I will be held to a greater accountability because of my calling. But religious people tend to read their own headlines too much, and then expect others to treat them differently as a result. Burdensome expectations follow quickly behind, or as Jesus said, *"heavy burdens on men's shoulders (Matt. 23:4a NASB)."*

I know a man who wants to be called "Apostle," another who has claimed the title "Bishop," and countless others who plant "Reverend" in front of their name as if their job makes them holier than others. I understand the importance of titles, especially those earned through hard work and sacrifice, but religious titles should be used to free people from burdens, not lay more on.

Leaders are the gatekeepers of the Kingdom. They are the ones who provide open doors and safe passage into the presence of God when the church gathers. If we are not careful, a desire to be approved can get in the way of the calling we've been given. Many people are so loaded up with burdens that they cannot enter into rest, into the Sabbath of the Lord. Don't add to it, okay? Instead, lead by example and leave the respectful greetings behind. They will only interrupt the Sabbath that the Lord desires for us all to have.

"Don't allow any loads into the gate on the Sabbath (Jer. 17:24 NASB)." It sounds like we've got our work cut out for us as leaders.

Family Time

Selah

On this day, talk with your family about the need for balance – a balance in celebrating accomplishments, hard work and achievement, with a prideful desire to be noticed, valued, and esteemed by others. Ask everyone in the family to name their favorite trophy, award or accomplishment. Celebrate the hard work that these items represent. Now explain that in Jesus's day, the religious leaders expected recognition and honor without earning it. Talk about what this might look like in today's culture. Would you want to be that kind of person? Why or why not?

Lord, I confess to you that I bear loads on this, Your Sabbath. In faith, I roll these heavy burdens on You today. Thank You that You exchange my burden with one that is light today.

Day Thirty-Four

"...God, who cannot lie, promised..." (Titus 1:2)
...so there remains a Sabbath rest for the people of God." (Heb. 4:9 NASB)

Are you tired of the struggle? Do you look about and suppose that the God who loves you has chosen to bless others with good gifts and you only with pain?

Fear not, you're in good company. Not one life that is cataloged by faith throughout the Bible had an easy life. Instead, we read about lives that are marked by struggle, loss, pain and failure yet punctuated with the exclamation, "But God!" The litany of the faithful reads like a tragic tale of loss but for God who intervenes and shows Himself to be strong by turning trials into triumphs.

God has promised you rest and He cannot lie. Though you are bruised by the cold stones that catch your feet on what seems an endless trek, God has promised and cannot lie. Though you lie down in tears and hear only the lies of the evil one telling you that life will never change, God has promised and cannot lie. Every step you take is closer to His glory so keep your eyes focused ahead and remember, God has promised and cannot lie!

There has never been a time like the one in which we now live. There has never been more wealth, more leisure, nor has there ever been more of an epidemic of depression, suicide, and self-destruction than in today's world. Could the two be linked together in some unseen diabolical plan of disaster? And could God's plan be that through trials the true saints would come to know His rest in the company of such realities so that others might come into a true peace and rest with Him as well?

The Sabbath spoken of by Jesus only begins here. The Sabbath is a well-worn path through the valleys, deserts, and mountains of this life that delivers us to the great celestial city of God. And though we strive to enter His rest, we are promised the companionship and protection of His Holy Spirit, our spiritual Sherpa that can be trusted. We might feel lost but He is not! Whatever path you are on, is the path today ordered by the Lord. Phillips Brooks said, "Faith says not, 'I see that it is good for me, so God must have sent it,' but, 'God sent it, and so it must be good for me.'"

There is a choice in rest. Do I choose to rest in God's ultimate plan and provision or strive to provide beyond the Master's release? Choose well, friend. Choose to trust in God.

Family Time

Selah

Remind your family that we have a God who always, always keeps His promises. In fact, Titus 1:2 says this plainly, *"God, Who cannot lie, promised..."*

So if God makes a promise, it's out of His character to break that promise. Here are some of the promises that God will always keep. Talk about the ones that bring you the most peace. "I'm grateful for God's promise that says—"

- As children of God, we can rejoice that our names are written in heaven (Luke 10:20 NASB).

- God will meet all our needs according to His glorious riches in Christ Jesus (Philippians 4:19 NASB).

- *"If we confess our sins, He is faithful and just and will forgive us our sins and purify us from all unrighteousness (1 John 1:9 NIV)."*

- We can approach the throne of grace with confidence, so that we may receive mercy and find grace to help us in our time of need (Hebrews 4:16 NASB).

Circumstances, Lord, circumstances! Things beyond my control are never beyond Your hand of providential love. I take my hand from what I cannot control and place it in Your loving hand. I choose to rest in You.

Day Thirty-Five

"The Son of Man is Lord of the Sabbath." (Matt. 12:8 NASB)

The Sabbath was what definitively separated the Jew from every other people group. It was not just a break in the week or a day off. It was an invitation from God to be separated totally to Him. Yahweh would provide. Yahweh would strengthen and bless. Yahweh would take thought of His people as His people took thought of Him. Other religions had temples, ceremonies, even circumcision, but no other religion had Sabbath as a seal of separation to their God.

Religion falsely promises that our efforts and rules will provide for us. That is why the Pharisees were so condemning of the behavior of the disciples. And that is why Jesus's words altered forever the relationship between the Sabbath and man. No longer would men earn their moral keep with rules. Having a relationship with the Lord of the Sabbath would win the day.

Religion lacks mercy. Religion profanes the heart qualities of God, and drains the life out of ceremony and ritual. Jesus said to them, *"If you had known what this means, 'I desire compassion and not a sacrifice,' you would not have condemned the innocent (Matt. 12:7 NASB)."*

He was not stating that God was permissive in His holy ways, but instead that the Sabbath of the Lord was designed around the compassion and mercy of God, and not the self-sacrifice of man. And as it was at the edge of that grain field, it is today. Jesus, the Lord of the Sabbath, desires to give you compassion and mercy in your hunger today. Sabbath sets the table with the best of God's provision.

So eat well today, traveler. May the Lord of the Sabbath fill your soul with His goodness and mercy.

Family Time

Selah

Sometimes we need practical ideas to "do" in order to learn how to "be" with one another. So set aside this time to listen and know one another more deeply. Ask one person in the family to hold some kind of ball or stuffed animal. Whoever is holding this item receives everyone else's undivided attention. Invite each family member to complete these sentences—

- The most important thing about me is *(blank)*.

- I feel loved in my family when *(blank)*.

- If you really knew me, you would know *(blank)*.

- I know I'm important to this family when *(blank)*.

Make this a time of rest. Make this a time to learn about one another. Make this a positive experience of knowing each other in new ways.

Lord, my prayer today is from Your word. "Good and upright is the Lord; Therefore He teaches sinners in the way. The humble He guides in justice, And the humble He teaches His way. All the paths of the Lord are mercy and truth, to such as keep His covenant and His testimonies" (Psalm 25:8-10 NKJV). Show me Thy way, O Lord of the Sabbath.

Day Thirty-Six

"The word of the Lord came to Elijah saying, 'Go away from here and turn eastward, and hide yourself by the brook Cherith...' and the ravens brought him bread and meat in the morning and bread and meat in the evening, and he would drink from the brook." (1 Kings 17:2-6 NASB)

Have you been sent to a desert to rest? So has Elijah. In today's world of retreats, spas and plush resorts set in the solitude of the desert, that might sound rather exotic, but Elijah's desert was not like that. It was just desert. Dry. Foreboding. Barren. Alone. It is likely that yours is the same.

The reason for the desert was two-fold. Elijah was on the run from the enemy who was trying to kill him. He was also worn out because of the intense season of spiritual battle he had fought. He was worn to the last spiritual bone and depressed to the point of "take my life." God's response was to send him to the desert.

God promised provision. Ravens, scavenger birds, not known for their generosity, were to bring the prophet food and the brook would give him water until, that is, the brook ran dry and the birds stopped coming. Sabbath can sometimes resemble a desert.

Sabbath is about God's provision, not God's comfort. His rest is better known in weakness than when my cup overflows with my own provision. Elijah experienced God's miraculous provision after he had exhausted his own resources and strength. It was in the desert that God chose to prove Himself. Sabbath, God's rest, was found at a dwindling brook and brought by ravens every day.

Do you find yourself at the brook Cherith? The word means "separation," by the way—the brook Separation, a time of life that is separated, cut off from others. Even though separated from others, you are not separated from God. He will even send His birds, the ravens, if necessary. But it is more likely that He will send His angels, friend. That's right. God will send His rest and provision on the wings of His angels to you.

Because even when we are so alone, God continues to provide His rest.

Family Time

Selah

Talk to your children about the "desert times" in your life. Tell the stories of hope - when life seemed dry and barren, but God miraculously provided. Talk to your kids about the times when life brought challenges, difficulties, and even pain, but God's ultimate provision prevailed. Our children need to know that faith in Jesus doesn't necessarily mean a life free from pain, but it does mean a life filled with God's provision. "Life was hard when *(blank)*, but God provided by *(blank)*."

Thank you, Father, that the circumstances do not dictate Your care for me. You send Sabbath in every circumstance. Open my eyes to see Your sweet provision in my desert place today.

Day Thirty-Seven

*"Departing from there, He went into their synagogue.
And a man was there whose hand was withered." (Matt. 12:9-10 NASB)*

Jesus went from the grain field to the synagogue and was immediately confronted again by the legalism of the Pharisees.

They descended on a man with a withered hand knowing instinctively that the one they detested, Jesus would love. They asked Him, "Is it lawful to heal on the Sabbath?" The question overflowed with contempt because any sort of deformity was disallowed in their worship. Like the good lawyers they were, they knew the answer before they asked the question.

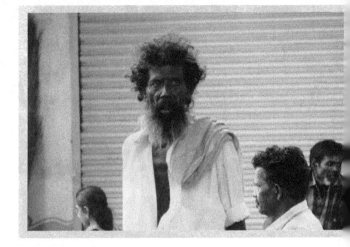

Jesus answered their question with a question, "If you have a sheep in a ditch, will you not pull it out, even on the Sabbath?" Not any sheep, mind you, but your sheep. Ownership was the issue, not sheep.

"How much more valuable than a sheep is a man!" and He healed the man's hand. Jesus had told them in the grain field that He was the Lord, the owner of the Sabbath. Now He declared that He was the owner of man. If they would rescue their own livestock from a ditch, how much greater good to rescue and set this man free.

It is difficult to come into Sabbath rest if you are mangled in some area of your life. That is why Jesus, the Lord of the Sabbath and the Lord of mankind, heals and sets free.

Isaiah said, *"To the eunuchs who keep My Sabbaths...even to them I will give in My house and within My walls a place and a name better than that of sons and daughters; I will give them an everlasting name that shall not be cut off (Isa. 56:4-5 NKJV)."*

Does the thought of holy ground like the Sabbath, and the talk of eunuchs make you uncomfortable? It should. The realities of ancient cultures are assaulting and cruel beyond measure. There were few physical blights that were greater than this. That is why it was used to demoralize and destroy entire cultures. That is why God says even these whose name would soon be forgotten would find rest in God's Sabbath.

God promises that He will even bless those whose future has been completely destroyed with a place and a name not to be cut off. Whether it be the withered soul or a lost destiny, Jesus, the Lord of the Sabbath, promises a hope and a future. Are you in need of Sabbath today? Reach out your hand. Jesus promises to heal. He is the Lord of the Sabbath and the Lord of your soul.

Family Time

Selah

Read the story of Matthew 12:9-13 with your family. Talk about the man with the withered hand, the Pharisees trickery, and the miracle of Christ's healing. Now with appropriate levels of vulnerability, share the areas of your life that God has miraculously healed. You may not have experienced the healing miracle of a withered hand, but have you been healed from anger, bitterness, fear, worry, or doubt? Share the story of your healing with your family. "God has restored my life in special ways just like the man with the withered hand. God has *(blank)*."

Lord, to You I turn and to You I appeal. All around me is the brokenness of sin and disease, but You promise restoration and healing in Your Sabbath. Come, Lord Jesus, I await Your touch.

Day Thirty-Eight

"...God blessed the seventh day and sanctified it, because in it He rested from all His work which God had created and made." (Gen. 2:3 NKJV)

It is a common thought, so old that it has earned the title of tradition. The Jewish sages noted it first in their writings about the Sabbath and many have written of it since. It is this: each of the six days of creation ends with the finality of "it was evening and the morning." The Jewish day would begin at sunset and end when three stars were visible the following twilight. It began in darkness and ended in darkness, the day caught between the bookends of night.

But the seventh day was different. The final day, God's day of rest, began but did not end as the other days. The scriptures separate it from the other days by the word *sanctify,* meaning to set apart for a special purpose. The purpose of that seventh day was that God rested from all His works. All of creation was finished. All that was created was "very good." According to the sages, the day was never meant to end.

What was left to be created were the children of Adam and Eve. In unity with God and one another, the two would become one. As an extension of the creative power found only in the Godhead, the children of Eden would be created. It was all good, friend. Very good.

Life would be the Sabbath of God, an unending peace, a symphony for the ages of blissful harmonic order that would emulate from every rock, tree, animal and even the sweet Garden air that they breathed. It was to be the eternal Sabbath of God, and the seventh day would never end. What had been created on that day would be the position of man resting in the everlasting arms of God.

The writer of Hebrews said, *"There remains therefore a rest for the people of God (Heb. 4:9 NKJV)."*

Spoken to the church, it was a promise that beyond salvation was a life to be attained that looked more like the Garden than the world in which we live. It is the life of Sabbath, a continual trust in the provision of God that breaths out the peace of God and inhales back His mercies. Sabbath is not a day or an event, it is a lifestyle promised yet only obtained if we choose to enter in.

And you are invited. Sabbath awaits you today or tonight or this afternoon or weekend. Because God's plan was for His children to always know His rest, even in the midst of this tribulation we call life.

Family Time

Selah

Remind your children of the creation story. Read Genesis 1-2, and marvel at the brilliance of God's plan for creation. Why did God create light before He created the plants? Why did He create plants before animals? God worked hard, and then He rested. Talk with your family about the work, plans and things to be done this week. Then celebrate your opportunity to rest. Set time aside, get it on the calendar. Set apart this time to rest and be together as a family – sanctify it.

"On *(blank)*, we're going to be together as a family. This time will be special and set apart for us."

Father, this noisy world screams turmoil and You call me to peace. I choose Your voice today and enter into rest. Thank You that You hold me in Your everlasting arms!

Day Thirty-Nine

"Speak also to the children of Israel, saying: 'Surely My Sabbaths you shall keep, for it is a sign between Me and you throughout your generations, that you may know that I am the Lord who sanctifies you.'" (Exo. 31:13 NKJV)

Go ahead. In fact, I dare you to say it. Go ahead and say that the Sabbath is just another old dead law that only a legalist would bother with. Go ahead and think of it as a suggestion or a dead tradition or something that is no longer really doable or even, dare I say, normal.

No doubt you have a point. There is not a day in the week where things really slow down. One of the two busiest days at airports is now Sunday, because of business people getting a jump on the work week. Slowly, the Sabbath has been eaten by commerce. You simply cannot mix the two because our greed will always overcome our humility.

But it is not a law. It is not a dead tradition. The Sabbath began in the perfection of new creation holiness. It was the culmination of gifts, the very best of God. The law came because the former slaves of Egypt needed rules to become human again. Four hundred years of bondage had destroyed both sanity and reason, so God spoke from His heart and said, "I will provide, I will care, I will love you well—and you rest."

Beyond the arguments about law and grace, there is so much more—in fact there is a great promise. Go ahead and say no to the Sabbath, but before you do, take time to think about the promise. God says that through Sabbath He will invoke a perpetual covenant. It means an everlasting guarantee.

When we sabbath, we are appealing to the everlasting guarantee of God's provision in every area of life - body, soul, and spirit. And through that perpetual covenant promised by God, His children are noted as different, distinguished and holy. Sabbath is what sanctifies, sets apart, marks as different, transforms the people of God. Not music, dress, speech or buildings—but Sabbath.

Sabbath is not just a day. It is not about twenty-four hours on a clock, or whether it begins at sunset or sunrise. Like every other redeemed promise, it is a matter of the heart. If my heart is truly trusting God then I am at rest, the perpetual rest that the writer of Hebrews spoke of. When I am at rest in the Lord, I simply don't struggle with the perpetual motion of business or busy-ness.

And now you must choose. Will you trust the everlasting guarantee of God, or are work and play and people and toys, and schedules and on and on and on so important that you must trust yourself. I, for one, just want to rest.

Family Time

Selah

Have a little fun with your kids and teach an object lesson at the same time. Choose a simple chore that's frequently done around your house like sweeping the floor or dusting the furniture. Now ask your children to act out this chore in several ways. How would it look if we did this chore at fast forward speed (Like a DVR or DVD)? At "2x fast forward speed"? At "4x fast forward speed?" In super slow motion? At a regular, normal pace?

Next, ask your children to give their input. When we go about our lives as a family, what speed does it feel like we are on? What speed would you like to be on? Discuss everyone's perspective and changes they would like to make.

Lord, reveal to my heart the perpetual covenant of Sabbath! I want to know You, Lord. What better way than to know Your promises. Thank You for loving me very well today.

Day Forty

"And he showed me a pure river of water of life, clear as crystal, proceeding from the throne of God and of the Lamb. In the middle of its street, and on either side of the river, was the tree of life, which bore twelve fruits, each tree yielding its fruit every month. The leaves of the tree were for the healing of the nations. And there shall be no more curse, but the throne of God and the Lamb shall be in it, and His servants shall serve Him. They shall see His face, and His name shall be on their foreheads. There shall be no night there; they need no lamp nor light of the sun, for the Lord God gives them light. And they shall reign forever and ever." (Rev. 22:1-5 NKJV)

We began *A Sabbath Rest* with the first prayer that Jesus taught us, and will end with the answer to the prayer in the Revelation of John. The divine seer and friend of Jesus saw a day when a better dawn than Adam's would break on God's creation. The place he saw was not Eden, far better than that in fact, but it certainly resembled what must have been in God's garden. There was a crystal clear river and the tree of life, safely transplanted in God's sight. And God was there. It is as if God chose His favorite furnishings from the Garden and brought them to heaven for safe keeping.

Look how all of time is turned back. The beauty of new creation is present. The tree of life is gloriously in bloom. The river runs crystal clear. All of these have the mark of the Garden. But the most emotional part of the passage is the seven words that ring back through the centuries to the terrible day of Adam's demise. On that day, Adam heard the unthinkable, *"Cursed is the ground for your sake."* But on this new day of everlasting that John tastes in his vision he records, *"And there shall be no more curse."*

In seven words, the number of perfection, He returns the perpetual state of the Sabbath rest. And we, the chosen of God, live in the middle. Not suffering the full curse of Adam for, *"[He became] a curse for us (Gal. 3:13 NKJV)."* Yet living as sojourners in a foreign land, looking for that city whose foundation is the Lord. Sabbath for us is available but we must strive to enter in.

And strive we must. Sabbath must be a lifestyle. We must use it to intrude on this world's agenda. We must teach it to our children and practice, practice, practice it in our lives. For Sabbath is where God resides and that is where we want to be. On that day, when heaven and earth pass and a new heaven and earth appears (Rev. 21:1 NASB), we shall know the rest that Adam knew on that first day. I, for one, look with great anticipation and wonder on that day. *"And God will wipe away every tear from their eyes; there shall be no more death, nor sorrow, nor crying. There shall be no more pain, for then former things have passed away. Then He who sat on the throne said, "Behold, I make all things new." (Revelation 21:4-5 NKJV)*

Maranatha! Come Quickly, Lord of the Sabbath!

Family Time

Selah

For this final time of Sabbath devotion, talk about the changes that the Sabbath reflections have meant to you personally and to your family. Talk about the before and after testimony of your lives together. As you summarize your thoughts, write your "before" and "after" testimonies onto cards or poster board. Write your "before" story on one side of the card. Write your "after" summary on the other side of the card. Your cards might look like this:

- Side #1 – "I thought I had to earn God's love."
  Side #2 – "Now I am resting in His love."

- Side #1 – "I thought that doing stuff was most important."
  Side #2 – "Now I know that being together is most important."

Share your before and after testimonies with another family. Celebrate in the Sabbath you see in one another's lives!

Remember the Sabbath Day, to keep it holy. Six days you shall labor and do all your work, but the seventh is the Sabbath of the Lord your God. In it you shall do no work; you, nor your son, nor your daughter, nor your male servant, nor your female servant, nor your cattle, nor your stranger who is within your gates. For in six days the Lord made the heavens and the earth, the sea, and all that is in them, and rested the seventh day. Therefore the Lord blessed the Sabbath day and hallowed it. (Exodus 20:8-11NKJV)

Epilogue

"I will give you rest." Matt. 11:28

Thank you for spending time learning about Sabbath, the great gift of God to His children. There is one final truth you need to know. Now that you've studied it, now that you've learned, now that "stop and rest" seems plausible, even attainable, now receive this rest as the gift of God.

How? By asking Jesus to take over your life and give you rest. True rest doesn't take hold until you invite the Lord of the Sabbath into your life. Until you do that, you can never know the gift of God that He has for you.

If you have never submitted your life to Jesus, here is how:

- Admit to God what you both know… He is right and you are wrong. He is holy and you are not. *"There is none righteous, not even one…there is none who seeks for God, all have turned aside… there is not who does good, not even one." Romans 3:10-12, NASB*

- Confess that you are incapable of dissolving your guilt and shame away. Tell Him you are a sinner incapable of saving yourself. *"All have sinned and fall short of the glory of God." Rom.2:2 NASB*

- Ask Jesus to forgive you of all your misdeeds, mistakes and sins. *"If you confess with your mouth Jesus as Lord and believe in your heart that God reaised Him from the dead, you will be saved." Romans 10:9*

- Give up control of your life to Jesus and declare Him Lord from this day forward. *"For God so loved the world, that He gave His only begotten Son, that whoever believes in Him shall not perish, but have eternal life." (John 3:16)*

- Ask the Holy Spirit to fill you with His transforming power. (John 20 and Acts 1)

- Rejoice and thank God that He has done what you have asked!

Find a church that tells the truth about the Bible and a group of people that are serious about a lifestyle modeled after Jesus. Talk to God (that is what prayer is) and read His word. Ask the Holy Spirit to speak to you.

Welcome to the family!

What Others Are Saying...

With insightful reflections and a passion for intimacy, my friend Dennis draws the reader into a journey of rest. In our frantic world of pseudo-relationships, nothing is more important than "practicing His Presence" and this well written and practical resource launches the reader into this exciting lifestyle. Read it and REAP!

David, Ferguson, D.Phil, D.Litt, LPC
Great Commandment Institute

In the richest of lands, we are often the poorest of peoples. We are so busy, but too often, we accomplish nothing of lasting value. Sadly, this is true not only of those around us, but also of the people of God. Is the rise of evil around us due to the fact that we as believers in Christ do not truly abide in Him? Yes, we go to church, we are involved in "His work" but we take little precious time with Him. This is true of all of us.
This book gives you an opportunity to break through the religiosity and the outward duties of "church work" and life's rat race to spend time with your Father in Heaven. That's what God intended for the Sabbath from the beginning–and opportunity to take time off and get to know Him and be refreshed by Him.
Come with expectation of a 40-day adventure, and let this wisdom-packed book lead you into the next and best period of your entire life!

Reverend Dr. T. Valson Abraham
Founder/President, India Gospel Outreach
Director, India Bible College and Seminary

I am a strong believer that a change of pace and a change of place gives new and needed perspective. In "A Sabbath Rest", Dennis wisely leads us in slowing the pace and finding that place of quiet rest, near the heart of God.
As the Sabbath day was a launch into a new week, "A Sabbath Rest" could be your launch into a new life.

Mark Batterson
New York Times best selling author of The Circle Maker
Lead Pastor of National Community Church

About The Author

Dennis and his wife, Jan, have pursued ministry together since 1977. For over 25 years, they have served the congregation of Freedom Fellowship Church in New Braunfels, Texas. Dennis is also an adjunct professor at India Bible College and Seminary where he teaches Relational Ministry and Pastoral Counseling. His travels have taken him extensively throughout the world which lends to his writing and speaking responsibilities. He currently blogs at ActLikeMenBlog.com and DennisGallaher.com.

CPSIA information can be obtained
at www.ICGtesting.com
Printed in the USA
LVHW05s0405140618
580519LV00001B/1/P